Grounded: A Comprehensive Guide to Grounding Techniques for Chilc Adults is a deeply personal and insightful memoir that chronicles . , decade-long career dedicated to supporting children and families on their journey towards healing and resilience. I have worked in the structured environment of a school, where I embarked on a path that would lead me to become a mental health play therapist, utilising the transformative principles of grounding techniques.

Throughout the pages of this book, readers are invited on a profound exploration of the challenges, triumphs, and lessons learned while working closely with children and families. My experiences from my own childhood and from the classroom to the therapy room have shaped my understanding of child development, trauma, and the power of connection.

As a mental health play therapist, I have delved into the world of play as a therapeutic tool, discovering its profound ability to unlock emotions, facilitate healing, and foster resilience in children facing adversity. Guided by the principles of grounding techniques, I have witnessed firsthand the transformative impact of providing a safe and nurturing space for children to explore and express themselves.

But my journey didn't stop there. Recognising the integral role of families in a child's healing process, I embrace a holistic approach that extends beyond the therapy room. Through collaboration, empathy, and empowerment, I work alongside families as a mental health play therapist to create a supportive environment where healing can flourish.

Grounded: A Comprehensive Guide to Grounding Techniques for Children and Adults" is not just a memoir; it's a testament to the resilience of the human spirit and the power of compassion to inspire change. It's a reminder that, even in the face of adversity, there is hope, healing, and the possibility of a brighter tomorrow—for every child and family I've had the privilege to work with and serve.

If you would like to connect with me, whether you want to talk about this book or you think I might be able to help you or your child or children you work with related to mental health therapy, or if there is anything else you think I might be able to help you with, please email me: Horizonplaytherapy@gmail.com or go to my website: horizonplaytherapy.com

Grounded: A Comprehensive Guide to Grounding Techniques for Children and Adults

Introduction: Grounded in Well-being

Welcome to the transformative world of grounding techniques—a guide designed to bring balance, peace, and resilience to the lives of both children and adults. In the midst of our fast-paced and often chaotic existence, the importance of staying connected to the present moment cannot be overstated. This book is a compass navigating you through a journey of self-discovery, mindfulness, and empowerment.

Grounding is a holistic approach to well-being that spans generations, offering a set of practices designed to anchor us in the present and cultivate a sense of inner peace. Whether you are a parent seeking tools to guide your child through the challenges of growing up or an adult striving for emotional balance and mental clarity, this book is a resource that empowers you to foster a grounded and centred life.

The journey begins by unravelling the concept of grounding itself—what it means and why it is crucial for maintaining mental, emotional, and physical health. From there, we delve into a rich tapestry of techniques tailored for children and adults, recognising the diverse needs and experiences each age group brings to the table.

For children, grounding becomes a whimsical adventure, a journey into the world of imagination, play, and sensory exploration. We explore activities that not only help them manage their emotions but also lay the foundation for a resilient and adaptable future. As we guide them through these techniques, we nurture their ability to face the world with curiosity, creativity, and emotional intelligence.

Adults, too, find solace in grounding—a sanctuary amid the demands of daily life. From simple yet powerful breathing exercises to the therapeutic benefits of nature, this guide is a roadmap to cultivating mindfulness, reducing stress, and fostering emotional well-being. Grounding techniques empower adults to navigate the complexities of their lives with grace, intention, and a profound sense of self-awareness.

As you embark on this journey, remember that grounding is not a destination; it is a continuous exploration. Each technique is a tool in your toolkit, offering a unique way to ground yourself in the present moment. Whether you are seeking moments of calm amidst chaos, tools for emotional regulation, or a path to self-discovery, this book is here to support you.

Embrace the journey ahead, discover the grounding techniques that resonate with you, and witness the positive impact they can have on your life. May this guide be a source of inspiration, empowerment, and a reminder that, in every breath and every moment, you have the power to cultivate a grounded and balanced life.

Chapter 1: Understanding Grounding

In the hustle and bustle of our modern lives, filled with constant demands and distractions, it's easy to feel overwhelmed and disconnected. The concept of grounding offers a profound antidote, a way to anchor ourselves in the present moment and cultivate a sense of inner stability. In this chapter, we embark on a journey to unravel the essence of grounding, exploring what it means and why it is a fundamental aspect of well-being for children and adults.

Defining Grounding:

At its core, grounding is a practice that involves bringing attention to the present moment and creating a connection between mind and body. It is a conscious effort to centre ourselves, fostering a sense of stability and balance. Whether through breathwork, sensory exploration, or mindful activities, grounding techniques act as a bridge that links us to the here and now.

Grounding, in the context of our exploration, is the transformative practice of tethering oneself to the present moment, creating a bridge between the internal landscape of thoughts and emotions and the external reality. It serves as an anchor in the currents of daily life, offering a sanctuary of stability amid the unpredictable waves of experience. Grounding techniques, designed for children and adults, aim to cultivate mindfulness, enhance self-awareness, and provide invaluable tools for emotional regulation. At its essence, grounding is the art of connecting with the here and now, fostering a deepened sense of security, balance, and resilience. Whether through mindful breathing, sensory engagement, or other intentional practices, grounding empowers individuals to navigate the ebb and flow of emotions, creating a foundation for sustained mental and emotional well-being. This book will serve as a guide to unlock the potential of grounding techniques, unveiling their transformative power for individuals of all ages.

The Importance of Grounding:

Why is grounding so crucial in the context of our well-being? As we navigate the challenges of daily life, stressors, and emotional fluctuations, grounding provides a refuge—a momentary pause that allows us to regain composure. It serves as a tool for emotional regulation, stress reduction, and overall mental clarity. Understanding the significance of grounding lays the foundation for integrating these practices into our daily routines.

Grounding is an indispensable practice that holds profound significance for enhancing mental and emotional well-being in both children and adults. At its core, grounding fosters a connection between individuals and the present moment, serving as a stabilising force amid the chaos of modern life. Individuals can anchor themselves to the present reality by engaging in grounding techniques, thereby alleviating stress, anxiety, and overwhelming emotions. This connection with the present not only cultivates mindfulness but also promotes a sense of security and balance.

For children, grounding techniques play a pivotal role in their emotional development, offering a valuable toolset to navigate the complexities of growing up. By fostering a strong foundation of self-awareness and emotional regulation, grounding empowers children to cope with challenges, build resilience, and forge healthier relationships. Moreover, grounding serves as a nurturing bridge between the child's inner world and external experiences, facilitating a more harmonious integration of thoughts and feelings.

In the realm of adulthood, grounding becomes an essential coping mechanism for the demands of daily life. As individuals face the pressures of work, relationships, and societal expectations, grounding provides a refuge—an oasis of serenity. It enables adults to cultivate a deeper understanding of their emotions, manage stress effectively, and maintain a stable mental state. The importance of grounding in adulthood lies in its ability to act as a steady anchor, preventing the turbulence of life from derailing emotional well-being.

In this comprehensive guide on grounding techniques for children and adults, we will explore a diverse array of methods, ranging from mindfulness practices to sensory grounding exercises and affirmations. By incorporating these techniques into daily routines, individuals can embark on a journey towards enhanced mental and emotional well-being, fostering resilience, balance, and a profound connection with the present moment.

The Mind-Body Connection:

Grounding techniques operate on the principle of the mind-body connection. By directing our focus to the sensations in our bodies, the rhythm of our breath, or the sights and sounds around us, we align our mental and physical states.

The mind-body connection forms the cornerstone of our understanding and application of grounding techniques for children and adults. It underscores the profound interplay between mental and physical well-being, recognising that our thoughts and emotions are intrinsically linked to the state of our bodies. Grounding, in essence, becomes a conduit for harmonising this intricate relationship, allowing individuals to synchronise their mental and physical realms. Through intentional practices such as deep breathing, gentle movement, and sensory engagement, we unlock the potential to create a cohesive balance between mind and body. This synergy not only enhances self-awareness but also empowers individuals to navigate challenges with resilience. In this book, we delve into the symbiotic nature of the mind and body, offering a comprehensive guide to utilising grounding techniques as a bridge to foster holistic well-being for both the cognitive and physical aspects of our existence.

Beyond Relaxation:

While relaxation is a natural byproduct of grounding, its benefits extend far beyond a momentary sense of calm. Grounding techniques become tools for resilience, empowerment, and self-awareness. As we explore various methods throughout this book, keep in mind that grounding is not a one-size-fits-all solution. It is a customisable practice that can be adapted to individual preferences and needs.

Beyond relaxation lies the expansive realm of grounding techniques—a transformative journey for children and adults that extends far beyond the mere alleviation of stress. While relaxation is a valuable byproduct, grounding techniques offer a holistic approach to well-being, encompassing mental, emotional, and physical dimensions. These practices act as catalysts for self-discovery, fostering resilience, and enhancing the overall quality of life. Beyond the momentary calm they provide, grounding techniques become powerful tools for building emotional intelligence, fostering mindfulness, and promoting a deeper connection with oneself and the surrounding world. This book delves into the multifaceted benefits of grounding, inviting readers to explore the profound impact these techniques can have on their lives—unveiling a path towards relaxation and a more grounded, centred, and enriched existence.

Embarking on the Grounding Journey:

As we delve deeper into this exploration of grounding, keep an open mind and a willingness to embrace new perspectives. Grounding is not a destination but an ongoing journey of self-discovery and growth. By understanding the foundations of grounding, we pave the way for the following practical techniques—techniques that will empower both children and adults to live more intentionally, with a heightened awareness of the present moment.

Beyond mere relaxation, the essence of grounding techniques for both children and adults transcends tranquillity, offering a gateway to holistic well-being. While these techniques certainly bring about a sense of calm, their true power lies in their capacity to cultivate emotional resilience, nurture self-awareness, and instil a profound connection with the present moment. Grounding techniques become a dynamic framework for personal growth, empowering individuals to navigate the complexities of life with grace and mindfulness. Through intentional practices that extend beyond momentary relief, this book illuminates the transformative potential of grounding, guiding readers toward a journey of self-discovery, emotional balance, and a more grounded and enriched way of living. It beckons individuals to embrace the broader spectrum of benefits that grounding techniques offer—beyond relaxation, toward a fuller, more connected existence.

In the chapters ahead, we will explore a rich array of grounding techniques, tailoring them to children's and adults' unique experiences and developmental stages. Through breath, movement, and mindful activities, we will uncover the transformative power of grounding in shaping a balanced and centred life.

Chapter 2: The historical roots of grounding

The incorporation of grounding in mindfulness practices has historical roots in various contemplative traditions that have long recognised the importance of anchoring one's awareness in the present moment. Here is an overview of the history of grounding in mindfulness:

Ancient Eastern Traditions:

Buddhism:

- Mindfulness is a central aspect of Buddhist teachings. The Buddha emphasised mindfulness as a vital component of the Eightfold Path, encouraging individuals to cultivate awareness of their thoughts, emotions, and actions. Grounding in the present moment is inherent in mindfulness meditation practices.

Zen Buddhism:

- Zen Buddhism, which originated in China and later developed in Japan, strongly emphasises mindfulness and presence. Practices such as zazen (seated meditation) and kinhin (walking meditation) involve a deep connection with each moment, fostering a grounded awareness.

Yoga and Hindu Traditions:

- Mindfulness is integral to various yogic and Hindu traditions. The practice of dharana (concentration) and dhyana (meditation) involves grounding the mind in a single focus point, often the breath, a mantra, or an object.

Mindfulness in Western Context:

Jon Kabat-Zinn and Mindfulness-Based Stress Reduction (MBSR):

- In the late 20th century, Jon Kabat-Zinn, a pioneer in the field of mindfulness, developed the Mindfulness-Based Stress Reduction (MBSR) program. Kabat-Zinn's approach integrated mindfulness meditation with a focus on present-moment awareness, drawing on his understanding of Buddhist teachings. MBSR introduced mindfulness practices to a Western audience in a secular context.

Modern Mindfulness Practices:

Mindfulness Meditation:

- Mindfulness meditation, popularised in the West, often includes grounding techniques. Practitioners are encouraged to anchor their attention in the present moment, often using the breath as a focal point. This practice enhances awareness, clarity, and a sense of grounded presence.

Mindful Movement Practices:

- Mindful movement practices, such as mindful walking and mindful yoga, emphasise grounding in each movement. These practices encourage individuals to be fully present and connected with the sensations and movements of the body.

Mindful Eating:

- Mindful eating involves grounding oneself in the sensory experience of eating. Practitioners pay attention to the flavours, textures, and smells of food, fostering a deeper connection with the act of nourishment.

Mindfulness in Psychotherapy:

- Mindfulness has been integrated into various forms of psychotherapy, such as Mindfulness-Based Cognitive Therapy (MBCT) and Dialectical Behaviour Therapy (DBT). These therapeutic approaches use grounding techniques to help individuals manage stress, regulate emotions, and cultivate a mindful awareness of their thoughts and feelings.

Integration into Mainstream Wellness:

Corporate Mindfulness Programs:

- Many corporations and organisations have adopted mindfulness programs to enhance employee well-being and productivity. These programs often include grounding practices to help individuals manage stress and stay focused in high-pressure environments.

Mindfulness Apps and Resources:

- The rise of mindfulness apps and online resources has made grounding practices more accessible to a broader audience. These platforms often offer guided meditations and exercises that emphasise staying grounded in the present moment.

The history of grounding in mindfulness reflects the integration of ancient contemplative traditions with modern approaches to well-being. Mindfulness, with its grounding practices, continues to evolve and find applications in various aspects of contemporary life, contributing to the promotion of mental and emotional health.

Chapter 3: Why use grounding exercises

Grounding exercises are used for various reasons, primarily to promote mental and emotional well-being by fostering a sense of connection and presence in the current moment. Here are some key reasons why grounding exercises are beneficial:

1. Anxiety Reduction:

Grounding techniques are effective in reducing anxiety by bringing attention to the present moment and diverting focus from anxious thoughts.

2. Stress Management:

Grounding exercises help manage stress by encouraging a shift in focus away from stressors, allowing individuals to regain control over their thoughts and emotions.

3. Mindfulness Promotion:

Grounding promotes mindfulness, which involves being fully present and engaged in the current experience without judgment. This can enhance overall mental clarity and well-being.

4. Emotional Regulation:

By grounding in the present moment, individuals can regulate their emotions more effectively, preventing overwhelming feelings and impulsive reactions.

5. Trauma Coping:

Grounding techniques are often used in trauma therapy to help individuals reconnect with the present and create a sense of safety when memories or triggers arise.

6. Improved Concentration:

Grounding exercises can enhance concentration and focus by redirecting attention from distractions to the immediate environment.

7. Body Awareness:

Many grounding exercises involve tuning into bodily sensations, fostering a greater awareness of one's physical state and promoting relaxation.

8. Interrupting Negative Thought Patterns:

Grounding techniques interrupt negative thought patterns and help individuals break free from cycles of rumination or obsessive thinking.

9. Self-Soothing:

Engaging in grounding activities can provide a sense of comfort and self-soothing during times of distress, helping individuals manage challenging emotions.

10. Enhanced Self-Connection:

Grounding exercises encourage self-connection and self-awareness, allowing individuals to better understand their thoughts, feelings, and reactions.

11. Preventing Overwhelm:

When faced with overwhelming situations, grounding techniques provide a way to stay anchored in the present and prevent feeling inundated by stressors.

12. Improved Sleep:

Grounding exercises can promote relaxation, making them useful for individuals struggling with insomnia or sleep difficulties.

13. Increased Resilience:

Regular grounding techniques contribute to increased emotional resilience, enabling individuals to navigate challenges more effectively.

14. Mind-Body Harmony:

Grounding fosters a connection between the mind and body, promoting a sense of harmony and balance.

15. Encouraging Present-Centered Living:

Grounding exercises emphasise the importance of living in the present rather than dwelling on the past or worrying about the future, fostering a more balanced perspective.

Whether used as part of stress management, coping with trauma, or simply promoting overall well-being, grounding exercises offer practical tools for individuals to stay connected, centred, and resilient in the face of life's challenges.

Chapter 4: What happens when a child or adult is not grounded

When a child or adult is not grounded, it can have various psychological, emotional, and physical consequences. Grounding, in the context of mental health and well-being, refers to being connected to the present moment, one's surroundings, and one's own emotions. Here are some potential outcomes when an individual is not grounded:

1. Increased Anxiety:

Lack of grounding can contribute to heightened anxiety as the mind becomes more prone to wandering into future worries or past concerns.

2. Difficulty Coping with Stress:

Without grounding techniques, individuals may find it challenging to cope with stressors effectively, leading to feelings of overwhelm.

3. Impaired Emotional Regulation:

The ability to regulate emotions may be compromised, making it challenging to manage intense or fluctuating feelings.

4. Disconnected Relationships:

When not grounded, individuals might struggle to be fully present in their relationships, leading to a sense of disconnection from others.

5. Rumination and Obsessive Thinking:

Ungrounded individuals may be more prone to rumination, dwelling on negative thoughts or scenarios, and engaging in obsessive thinking patterns.

6. Reduced Self-Awareness:

Lack of grounding can result in diminished self-awareness, making it harder for individuals to understand and navigate their own emotions and behaviours.

7. Impaired Concentration:

The ability to concentrate and focus on tasks may be compromised, affecting productivity and overall cognitive functioning.

8. Increased Reactivity:

Without grounding, individuals may react impulsively to situations, responding emotionally without thoughtful consideration.

9. Sleep Difficulties:

Lack of grounding can contribute to difficulties in winding down and relaxing, potentially leading to sleep disturbances.

10. Decreased Resilience:

Grounding is associated with emotional resilience. Without it, individuals may find it harder to bounce back from life's challenges.

11. Escapism Behaviours:

Some individuals may turn to unhealthy coping mechanisms such as substance abuse, excessive screen time, or other forms of escapism when they are not grounded.

12. Impaired Decision-Making:

The ability to make clear and reasoned decisions may be compromised when individuals are not grounded, potentially leading to poor choices.

13. Struggle with Mindfulness:

With grounding, individuals may engage in mindful practices, gaining the benefits of being in the moment. It's important to note that everyone may experience moments of being ungrounded, and occasional lapses in grounding are a normal part of life. However, persistent challenges with grounding may benefit from intentional practices and strategies to reconnect with the present moment and enhance overall well-being. Professional support from mental health professionals may be valuable for individuals facing chronic difficulties with grounding.

Chapter 5: The Basics of Grounding

In our quest for a balanced and centred life, understanding the fundamental principles of grounding is essential. This chapter serves as a gateway into the core techniques that lay the groundwork for a mindful and intentional existence. We will explore the simple yet powerful practices that form the bedrock of grounding, applicable to both children and adults.

1. Breathing Exercises:

At the heart of grounding lies the breath, a constant companion that can guide us back to the present moment. From the gentle rhythm of belly breathing to the structured 4-7-8 technique, mastering the art of conscious breathing is a foundational skill for grounding.

Within the tapestry of grounding techniques for children and adults, the rhythmic dance of breath takes centre stage as an indispensable thread. Breathing exercises serve as a universal language, a bridge between the internal and external realms, offering profound benefits for emotional well-being and mental clarity. From mindful breathing that calms racing thoughts to deep diaphragmatic breaths that release tension, these exercises become tools for self-regulation and a pathway to emotional balance. With each inhalation and exhalation, individuals embark on a journey of self-discovery, unlocking the transformative power of breath to alleviate stress, promote mindfulness, and cultivate a deeper connection with the self. This comprehensive guide illuminates the art of breathing exercises, inviting readers to explore and integrate these practices into their daily lives for a more grounded and centred existence.

The 4-7-8 breathing technique, also known as the Relaxing Breath, is a simple and effective method for reducing stress and promoting relaxation. Here's how to do it:

Sit or lie down in a comfortable position, with your back straight and your shoulders relaxed. You can also do this technique, standing up if that's more comfortable for you. Close your eyes gently to help you focus on your breath and block out distractions.

Relax Your Jaw: Let your jaw relax and part your lips slightly. You can rest the tip of your tongue against the roof of your mouth, just behind your front teeth, if that feels comfortable.

Inhale for 4 Seconds: Take a slow, deep breath in through your nose for a count of 4 seconds. Feel your lungs fill with air and your abdomen expand as you inhale.

Hold your breath for a count of 7 seconds. Try to keep your chest and abdomen relaxed as you hold your breath.

Slowly exhale through your mouth for a count of 8 seconds. As you exhale, imagine all the tension and stress leaving your body with each breath.

Repeat the cycle of inhaling for 4 seconds, holding for 7 seconds, and exhaling for 8 seconds. Continue the breathing pattern for several rounds, gradually deepening your breath and relaxing further with each repetition.

Practice the 4-7-8 breathing technique regularly, ideally twice a day or whenever you feel stressed or anxious. With practice, you'll become more skilled at using this technique to calm your mind and body in moments of stress.

The 4-7-8 breathing technique can help activate the body's relaxation response, reduce stress hormones, and promote a sense of calm and well-being. It's a simple yet powerful tool that you can use anytime, anywhere, to manage stress and improve your overall health and well-being.

2. Mindfulness Meditation:

Meditation is a timeless practice that invites us to cultivate awareness and presence. You can explore basic mindfulness meditation techniques suitable for beginners, emphasising the importance of being fully engaged in the current experience. These practices serve as anchors, allowing us to observe our thoughts without judgment and return to a state of centeredness.

Mindfulness meditation emerges as a beacon of introspection and serenity in the realm of grounding techniques for both children and adults. At its core, mindfulness meditation is a conscious and non-judgmental immersion into the present moment, a gentle exploration of one's thoughts and sensations. Whether guiding children through imaginative visualisations or assisting adults in finding calm amidst life's turbulence, mindfulness meditation offers a sanctuary for reflection and repose. Through the gentle cadence of breath and focused awareness, individuals embark on a transformative journey, learning to navigate the complexities of their inner world with grace and presence.

Mindfulness meditation

Sit in a comfortable position with your back straight but relaxed. You can sit on a cushion, a chair, or even on the floor. Close your eyes gently or soften your gaze, whichever feels more comfortable.

Bring your attention to your breath. Notice the sensation of the air flowing in and out of your nostrils or the rise and fall of your chest or abdomen as you breathe. There's no need to change your breath; simply observe it as it naturally occurs.

Acknowledge Thoughts and Feelings as you focus on your breath, thoughts, emotions, and bodily sensations that may arise. Acknowledge them without judgment or attachment, simply noticing them as they come and go. If your mind wanders, gently bring your attention back to your breath.

Return to the Present Moment: Whenever you notice your mind wandering or becoming distracted, gently return your focus to the present moment and your breath. Each time you bring your attention back, you're strengthening your ability to be mindful and present.

Practice this four-step mindfulness meditation for a few minutes each day, gradually increasing the duration as you become more comfortable with the practice. Remember, the key is to cultivate a non-judgmental awareness of your present experience, allowing thoughts and feelings to arise and pass without getting caught up in them. With regular practice, mindfulness meditation can help reduce stress, increase self-awareness, and promote overall well-being.

3. Progressive Muscle Relaxation:

Tension often accumulates in our bodies as a response to stress. Progressive muscle relaxation is a systematic method involving tensing and releasing different muscle groups. By heightening our awareness of physical sensations, we can unwind the body and, in turn, ease the mind. This technique is particularly beneficial for adults seeking relief from stress and physical tension.

Progressive Muscle Relaxation (PMR) is a practice that invites individuals to embark on a journey of self-discovery and relaxation by systematically tensing and then releasing different muscle groups. As the body unwinds, so does the mind, creating a harmonious synergy between physical and mental relaxation. Whether guiding children through a playful exploration of bodily sensations or assisting adults in releasing accumulated tension, PMR becomes a versatile tool for achieving a state of profound calm.

By engaging in this intentional and mindful process, individuals not only alleviate physical stress but also cultivate a heightened awareness of the mind-body connection, paving the way for a more grounded and serene existence. Through the gentle unravelling of muscle tension, this technique becomes a powerful ally in the quest for overall well-being, providing a pathway to tranquillity for individuals of all ages.

4. Visualization Techniques:

The power of the mind extends to the images we create within it. Visualisation techniques guide us to create mental images that evoke calmness and positivity. Whether envisioning a serene natural setting or picturing a place of personal significance, these techniques harness the imagination to foster a sense of peace and tranquillity.

Visualisation techniques, for children and adults, are like windows to the imagination, offering a transformative pathway to emotional well-being. Visualisation invites individuals to embark on a mental journey, exploring vibrant and calming imagery to foster a profound sense of connection and relaxation. Tailored for diverse age groups, there is a versatile world of visualisation techniques, guiding children through whimsical and imaginative landscapes and adults through scenes of tranquillity and empowerment.

Whether picturing a serene beach or envisioning a protective bubble of light, these techniques become powerful tools for grounding, as they allow individuals to escape momentarily from stress and reconnect with a deeper, more serene aspect of themselves. Through the vivid tapestry of the mind's eye, individuals of all ages can cultivate a sanctuary of peace, tapping into the limitless potential of visualisation to enhance their overall well-being and foster a lasting connection with inner calm.

Visualisation technique:

Find a quiet and comfortable space where you won't be disturbed. Sit or lie down in a relaxed position, close your eyes, and take a few deep breaths to centre yourself and release any tension in your body.

Visualise a specific scene or scenario in your mind's eye. It could be a place where you feel calm and peaceful, such as a tranquil beach, a serene forest, or a cosy room. Imagine the details of this scene as vividly as possible, including colours, textures, sounds, and smells.

Use your imagination to engage all of your senses in the visualisation. Notice the warmth of the sun on your skin, the sound of the waves crashing against the shore, the scent of the ocean breeze, and the feeling of the sand between your toes. Try to make the experience as lifelike and immersive as possible.

Stay present in the moment and fully immerse yourself in the visualisation. Allow yourself to experience a sense of relaxation, peace, and well-being as you connect with the mental image you've created. Enjoy the feelings of calmness and contentment that arise from this visualisation.

Practice this four-step visualisation technique regularly, especially during times of stress or when you need to relax and unwind. With practice, you'll become more adept at using visualisation as a tool for promoting relaxation, reducing stress, and enhancing overall well-being.

In this chapter, we lay the foundation for the diverse range of grounding techniques to follow. These basics are not merely introductory exercises but the building blocks upon which a more grounded life is constructed. As we journey through each technique, remember that the simplicity of these practices belies their profound impact. The basics of grounding provide us with a toolkit that can be accessed at any moment, empowering us to navigate the complexities of life with grace and mindfulness.

As we move forward and embrace these fundamental practices with an open heart and a curious mind. They are the keys to unlocking the transformative potential of grounding and guiding children and adults toward a more centred and purposeful existence.

Chapter 6: Key Concepts of Grounding Techniques

In the pursuit of holistic well-being, grounding techniques serve as transformative tools, guiding individuals toward a deeper connection with the present moment. This chapter explores the fundamental concepts underlying grounding techniques, shedding light on their significance in fostering emotional resilience, stress management, and an overall sense of balance in the fast-paced tapestry of modern life.

1. Mindfulness as a Foundation:

Present Moment Awareness: At the core of grounding techniques lies the principle of mindfulness—the practice of being fully present in the current moment. Grounding invites individuals to shift their focus away from past or future concerns and immerse themselves in the richness of the present.

2. Sensory Engagement:

Grounding techniques often involve sensory engagement, encouraging individuals to connect with their immediate surroundings. Whether through touch, sight, sound, smell, or taste, this concept heightens awareness and anchors individuals in the tangible aspects of the present moment.

3. Breath as an Anchor:

The breath serves as a powerful anchor in grounding techniques. The conscious act of breathing becomes a rhythmic, calming force that individuals can return to whenever they need to centre themselves. Breath awareness promotes relaxation and mental clarity.

Breath as an anchor:

Sit or lie down in a comfortable position, with your back straight but relaxed. Close your eyes gently or soften your gaze.

Bring your attention to your breath as it naturally flows in and out of your body. Notice the sensation of the breath entering and leaving your nostrils or the rise and fall of your chest or abdomen. Use the breath as your anchor to the present moment, allowing it to guide your attention away from distractions and into a state of mindfulness.

By focusing solely on the breath, you can cultivate a sense of calm and presence, even in the midst of chaos or stress. Practice this simple technique regularly to develop greater mindfulness and awareness in your daily life.

4. Connecting with the Body:

Grounding is an embodied experience, emphasising the connection between the mind and body. Techniques like body scans and progressive muscle relaxation facilitate an awareness of physical sensations, promoting relaxation and reducing tension.

Mindful movement, such as qigong, involves combining physical movements with focused attention and mindfulness:

Centre Yourself:

Find a quiet and comfortable space where you can stand or sit comfortably. Take a moment to centre yourself by bringing your awareness to your breath. Close your eyes if it feels comfortable, and take a few deep breaths to relax your body and mind.

Begin with gentle warm-up exercises to prepare your body for movement. This may include shaking out your hands and arms, rolling your shoulders, and gently twisting your torso from side to side. Allow your movements to be slow, deliberate, and mindful, paying attention to the sensations in your body as you warm up.

Practice Qigong Movements:

Choose a simple qigong sequence or set of movements to practice. Focus on each movement with mindfulness, paying attention to the sensations in your body, the flow of your breath, and the connection between your mind and body. Move slowly and gracefully, allowing your movements to be fluid and relaxed.

Close with Stillness:

After completing your qigong practice, take a moment to stand or sit quietly in stillness. Bring your attention back to your breath, noticing the sensations of your breath as it flows in and out of your body. As you conclude your practice, allow yourself to feel grounded, centred, and at peace.

By practising qigong in this mindful and intentional way, you can enhance your physical, mental, and emotional well-being, promoting relaxation, balance, and harmony within yourself.

5. Nature's Therapeutic Influence:

Grounding can often involve connecting with nature. Whether it's a walk in the woods, feeling the grass beneath one's feet, or simply gazing at the sky, nature provides a therapeutic backdrop that fosters a sense of calm, connection, and perspective.

Connect with Nature:

Spend time in natural settings such as parks, forests, beaches, or gardens. Engage your senses by noticing the sights, sounds, smells, and textures of the natural world around you. Take a leisurely walk, sit quietly by a body of water, or simply observe the beauty of your surroundings.

Practice Mindfulness:

Use nature as a backdrop for mindfulness practice. Bring your attention to the present moment by focusing on your breath, sensations in your body, or the sights and sounds of nature. Allow yourself to fully immerse in the experience without judgment or distraction.

Recharge and Relax:

Nature provides a tranquil and rejuvenating environment where you can recharge and relax. Take advantage of opportunities for rest and relaxation in natural settings, whether it's lounging in a hammock, picnicking under a tree, or simply basking in the warmth of the sun.

6. Creating Mental Sanctuaries:

Visualisation techniques tap into the power of imagination. By creating mental images of peaceful places or scenarios, individuals create a mental sanctuary that offers solace and serves as a retreat from the demands of daily life.

Create a Safe Space:

Within your mental sanctuary, create a sense of safety and protection. Imagine a bubble of light surrounding you, providing a shield of protection from external stressors and negative energies. Allow yourself to feel completely safe and secure within this space, knowing that you are protected and supported.

7. Personalized Grounding Objects:

Grounding objects, chosen for their tactile qualities, become anchors in the physical world. These objects provide a tangible focus, offering comfort and grounding through touch. The concept emphasises the importance of personalised tools for each individual.

8. Purposeful Attention:

Grounding encourages purposeful attention to the current experience. This concept extends beyond mere observation, urging individuals to fully engage with and immerse themselves in the details of the present moment.

Purposeful Attention:

Set Your Intention: Begin by consciously deciding to be present in the moment and to direct your attention purposefully. Decide to approach your experiences with openness, curiosity, and acceptance rather than being carried away by distractions or judgments.

Focus on Your Anchor:

Choose a focal point for your attention, such as your breath, a specific sensation in your body, or an object in your environment. Direct your attention to your chosen anchor and maintain your focus on it, using it as a tool to anchor yourself in the present moment. Whenever your mind starts to wander, gently bring your attention back to your anchor, reinforcing your intention to stay present.

By setting your intention and focusing on your chosen anchor, you can cultivate purposeful attention and develop greater mindfulness and presence in your daily life.

9. Body-Mind Connection:

Grounding techniques recognise the interconnectedness of the body and mind. By addressing both aspects, individuals nurture holistic well-being. Techniques that promote relaxation, such as progressive muscle relaxation, embody this concept.

The body-mind connection refers to the intricate relationship between our physical health and mental well-being:

Awareness of Sensations:

Begin by developing awareness of the sensations in your body. Notice how your physical sensations, such as tension, discomfort, or relaxation, are interconnected with your thoughts, emotions, and overall mental state. Pay attention to how stress, anxiety, or negative emotions can manifest as physical symptoms in the body and vice versa.

Practice Mind-Body Techniques:

Engage in practices that foster the integration of the body and mind, such as mindfulness meditation, yoga, tai chi, or qigong. These practices involve gentle movements, breath work, and meditation techniques that promote relaxation, stress reduction, and greater awareness of the body-mind connection. By incorporating these practices into your daily routine, you can cultivate a deeper understanding of how your physical and mental states influence each other and learn to optimise your health and well-being holistically.

10. Mindful Movement:

Grounding extends to mindful movement practices, such as yoga or tai chi. These activities integrate breath, movement, and mindfulness, offering a holistic approach to grounding that aligns the body and mind.

11. Incorporating Grounding into Daily Life:

Grounding is not solely an isolated practice; it thrives on consistency and integration into daily life. Establishing grounding rituals—whether morning routines, breaks during the day, or evening wind-downs—sustains its transformative impact.

12. Intention and Awareness:

Conscious Engagement: Grounding emphasises intentional and conscious engagement with the chosen technique. The concept underscores the importance of approaching grounding practices with awareness, fostering a deeper connection with the self and the surrounding environment.

In essence, the critical concepts of grounding techniques revolve around the citation of mindfulness, sensory awareness, and a conscious connection with the present moment. By embracing these concepts, individuals embark on a transformative journey that enhances their well-being, promotes resilience, and empowers them to navigate the complexities of life with grace and groundedness.

Chapter 7: Grounding Techniques for Children

Children, with their boundless curiosity and vivid imaginations, are uniquely poised to embrace the transformative power of grounding techniques. In this chapter, we explore the significance of adapting grounding practices to cater specifically to children's needs and developmental stages. From simple breathing exercises to imaginative adventures, these techniques aim to instil a foundation of emotional resilience, self-awareness, and joy in their lives.

1. The Importance of Adapting Grounding Techniques for Children:

Understanding that children experience the world differently than adults is fundamental. Grounding techniques tailored to their age and developmental stage not only capture their attention but also provide them with practical tools to navigate the challenges they encounter. By recognising and embracing their natural inclination towards play and imagination, we create a nurturing environment for their emotional growth.

The adaptation of grounding techniques for children is not just a short-term solution; it is an investment in their future well-being. By instilling these techniques early on, we nurture a foundation of skills that can serve them throughout their lives. The ability to ground themselves, manage emotions, and navigate challenges becomes an integral part of their personal toolkit for resilience and well-being.

Tailoring grounding techniques for children is an expression of understanding and empathy. It acknowledges that their world is distinct from the adult realm and requires unique tools. This understanding fosters trust, communication, and a sense of security, laying the groundwork for positive parent-child relationships and supportive educational environments.

In essence, the importance of adapting grounding techniques for children is a testament to our commitment to their holistic development. By recognising and embracing their innate playfulness, imagination, and unique challenges, we provide them with not just tools for the moment but skills that can shape a lifetime of emotional resilience, self-awareness, and well-being.

2. Simple Breathing Exercises for Kids:

Introducing children to mindful breathing can lay the groundwork for emotional regulation—child-friendly breathing exercises, transforming the act of breathing into an engaging and enjoyable activity. Techniques like "Bubble Breaths" and "Dragon Breaths" make the practice accessible and fun, enabling children to cultivate a sense of calmness and self-control.

"Dragon Breaths" is a mindfulness practice often utilised in yoga, meditation, and relaxation exercises. It involves a specific breathing technique that encourages deep, diaphragmatic breathing and helps release tension and stress from the body. Here's how to do it:

1. Find a Comfortable Position:

Sit or lie down in a comfortable position. Close your eyes if it feels comfortable to do so.

2. Take a Deep Breath In. Inhale deeply through your nose, filling your lungs with air. As you breathe in, expand your belly like a balloon, allowing it to rise and fill with air.

3. Exhale Slowly: Exhale slowly and steadily through your mouth. As you breathe out, purse your lips slightly and make a soft, audible sound like a gentle roar, similar to the sound of a dragon breathing out fire.

4. Repeat: Continue to take deep breaths in through your nose and out through your mouth, making the soft roaring sound with each exhale. Focus on the sensation of the breath entering and leaving your body.

5. Relax and Release Tension: As you practice Dragon Breaths, allow yourself to relax deeper with each exhale. Feel any tension or stress melting away with each breath out, leaving you feeling calm and grounded.

6. Continue for Several Breaths: Practice Dragon Breaths for several breaths, allowing yourself to fully immerse in the rhythm and flow of your breath. You can do this for as long as you like, but even just a few minutes can be beneficial for relaxation and stress relief.

Dragon Breaths can be particularly helpful for calming the mind, relieving anxiety, and promoting a sense of relaxation and well-being. It's a simple yet effective technique that can be practised anywhere, anytime, whenever you need a moment of peace and tranquillity.

3. Guided Imagery for Children:

The power of imagination becomes a guiding force in grounding techniques for children. Guided Imagery is where storytelling and visualisation transport children to a realm of calm and safety. These imaginative journeys serve as a bridge between the natural world and the world of their thoughts, fostering creativity and emotional well-being.

Title: The Magic Bubble

1. Introduction: "Close your eyes and take a deep breath in, filling your lungs with air. As you exhale, imagine a magic bubble forming around you. This bubble is made of shimmering light and is filled with love and protection."

2. Exploring the Bubble:

 "Inside the bubble, you feel safe and secure. It's like your own special sanctuary where nothing can harm you. Take a moment to explore the inside of the bubble, noticing how it glows with a soft, comforting light."

Closing:

"When you're ready, take one more deep breath in, feeling the warmth and love of the magic bubble surrounding you. Slowly open your eyes and carry the feeling of safety and protection with you as you go about your day."

This short, guided imagery script is designed to help children create a sense of safety and security within themselves, using their imagination to visualise a protective bubble of light around them. Feel free to adjust the script to suit the age and preferences of the children participating.

4. Creative and Playful Grounding Activities:

Grounding is not about rigidity; it thrives on creativity and play. Through activities that engage the senses, children discover the joy of being present. Sensory exploration, encompassing touch, sight, sound, smell, and taste, becomes a delightful avenue for grounding. Simple exercises like feeling different textures or identifying various scents heighten sensory awareness while making the process enjoyable.

Sensory Bottles or Bags:

Create sensory bottles or bags filled with different materials, such as:
Rice, beans, or sand for tactile stimulation
Sequins, glitter, or beads for visual stimulation
Essential oils or scented cotton balls for olfactory stimulation
Bells, marbles, or beans for auditory stimulation

Texture Exploration:
Provide a variety of textured objects for children to explore with their hands, such as:
Smooth stones
Fuzzy fabrics
Rough sandpaper
Bumpy rubber balls

Sensory Playdough:
Use scented or textured playdough to engage multiple senses while moulding and shaping:
Add essential oils for olfactory stimulation.
Mix in rice, beans, or sand for tactile stimulation.
Use food colouring for visual stimulation.

5. Nature Connection Activities:

The natural world holds a special allure for children. Grounding activities that involve connecting with nature, whether it's a walk in the park, observing the clouds, or simply feeling the earth beneath their feet. Nature becomes a teacher, imparting valuable lessons about presence, interconnectedness, and the beauty of the world around them.

6. Imaginary Adventures:

The power of imagination takes centre stage as we guide children through imaginary adventures. These exercises encourage creative expression, allowing children to visualise safe and comforting places in their minds. Imaginary adventures become a tool for emotional exploration, self-discovery, and building resilience.

Imaginary adventures involve using the power of your imagination to explore new worlds, situations, and possibilities. Here's how to embark on imaginary adventures in two steps:

Set the Scene:

Begin by creating a mental image of the adventure you'd like to experience. This could be anything from exploring a mystical forest, journeying to outer space, or going on a magical quest. Use your imagination to vividly visualise the details of your adventure, including the sights, sounds, smells, and sensations you might encounter along the way.

Engage Your Senses:

Once you've set the scene, fully immerse yourself in the adventure by engaging your senses. Imagine what it would feel like to walk through the forest, soar through the stars, or interact with fantastical creatures. Allow yourself to become fully absorbed in the experience, suspending disbelief and embracing the possibilities of your imagination.

By engaging in imaginary adventures, you can tap into your creativity, expand your imagination, and experience a sense of wonder and excitement that can inspire and uplift you. Whether you're looking for a brief escape from reality or a creative outlet for self-expression, imaginary adventures offer endless opportunities for exploration and discovery.

In this chapter, we lay the groundwork for fostering emotional intelligence and well-being in children through tailored grounding techniques. By embracing their innate playfulness and imagination, we equip them with the tools to navigate the journey of growing up with resilience, self-awareness, and a sense of wonder. Grounding becomes not just a practice but a delightful adventure for the young explorers of life.

Chapter 8 Grounding techniques for children with learning difficulties

Children with learning difficulties often face unique challenges that can impact their ability to regulate emotions, manage stress, maintain focus and regulate sensory input. Grounding techniques provide valuable tools to help these children navigate their daily experiences with greater ease and confidence, helping these children feel more centred, calm, and engaged in their environment. By understanding the importance of grounding techniques and tailoring them to the specific needs of children with learning difficulties, educators and caregivers can create supportive environments that foster emotional well-being and academic success.

Understanding Learning Difficulties:

Before delving into grounding techniques, it's essential to have a basic understanding of the various learning difficulties that children may face. These difficulties can range from attention deficit hyperactivity disorder (ADHD) and autism spectrum disorder (ASD) to specific learning disabilities such as dyslexia, dyscalculia, and auditory processing disorder. Each child's experience is unique, and their needs may vary based on their individual strengths and challenges.

The Impact of Learning Difficulties

Children with learning difficulties may experience a range of challenges, including difficulty processing information, maintaining attention, and regulating emotions. These challenges can lead to feelings of frustration, anxiety, and feeling overwhelmed, making it difficult for children to participate fully in classroom activities and social interactions. Grounding techniques offer practical strategies to help children manage these difficulties and develop essential coping skills.

Tailoring Grounding Techniques to Children with Learning Difficulties

Children with learning difficulties may have unique sensory preferences, communication styles, and emotional needs that require special consideration when implementing grounding techniques. It's essential to adapt grounding techniques to align with each child's strengths, challenges, and individual learning profiles. By tailoring grounding techniques to the specific needs of children with learning difficulties, educators and caregivers can maximise their effectiveness and promote positive outcomes.

Understanding the Importance of Grounding Techniques

Children with learning difficulties often face challenges with attention, focus, emotional regulation, and sensory processing. Grounding techniques provide valuable tools to help these children manage stress, regulate emotions, and enhance their ability to engage in learning and daily activities. In this chapter, we will explore a variety of grounding techniques, offering practical strategies to promote relaxation, sensory integration, and self-regulation.

Sensory Grounding Techniques

Tactile Grounding:

Sensory Bins: Create sensory bins filled with various textures, such as rice, beans, or sand, to provide tactile stimulation and sensory exploration.

Fidget Toys: Offer fidget toys or sensory balls to provide tactile input and promote self-regulation during times of stress or anxiety.

Visual Grounding:

Calming Visual Aids: Set up a calming sensory corner with visual aids such as lava lamps, bubble tubes, or calming pictures to create a visually soothing environment.

Visual Schedules:

Use visible schedules or picture cards to help children understand and navigate daily routines and transitions.

Auditory Grounding:

Noise Reduction Tools: Provide noise-cancelling headphones or earplugs to reduce auditory distractions and create a quiet space for learning and concentration.

Calming Sounds:

Play calming music or nature sounds in the background to promote relaxation and focus during tasks or activities at home or school.

Mindfulness and Relaxation Techniques

Breathing Exercises:

Belly Breathing: Teach children deep belly breathing techniques to help them calm their minds and bodies during moments of stress or overwhelm.

Belly breathing, also known as diaphragmatic breathing, is a breathing technique that involves breathing deeply into the abdomen rather than shallowly into the chest. It engages the diaphragm, a large muscle located below the lungs, to fully expand the lungs and allow for a more efficient exchange of oxygen and carbon dioxide.

Belly breathing is a technique where the child takes deep breaths using their belly instead of their chest. Here's how it works:

1. Ask the child to find a comfortable spot to sit or lie down.

2. Ask them to place one hand on their chest and one hand on their belly.

3. Ask them to take a slow, deep breath in through their nose. As they do, ask them to try to let their belly push out against their hand. Say, imagine filling up a balloon in your belly.

4. Ask them to hold their breath for a moment.

5. Ask them to slowly exhale through their mouth. Say, feel your belly go back in, like the balloon deflating.

Belly breathing helps you relax because it slows down your heart rate and helps you get more oxygen. It's like giving your body a little break and helping your mind feel calm. You can help the children do belly breathing whenever they feel stressed, anxious, or just want to relax. Practice it regularly, and it'll become more accessible and effective over time.

Square Breathing:

Introduce square breathing exercises, where children inhale for a count of four, hold for a count of four, exhale for a count of four, and hold for a count of four, repeating the cycle. Depending on the age and lung capacity or if the child has a medical condition, they may struggle to hold their breath for four seconds, so you may need to modify this number from four to three ...., depending on the child. For children with medical conditions, this may not be a safe grounding activity, so please seek medical advice.

Guided Imagery:

Lead children through guided imagery exercises that engage their imagination and promote relaxation, such as visualising themselves in a peaceful, serene setting. However, some children with special needs will struggle with imagination.

Underwater Adventure

Let's dive into an exciting underwater adventure! Close your eyes and imagine yourself swimming in the ocean, surrounded by colourful fish and swaying seaweed.

Picture yourself diving into the ocean, feeling the cool water surrounding your body. Can you feel the water tickling your skin?

Look around and see if you can spot any friendly sea creatures swimming nearby. Say hello to the sea creatures and see if they'll play with you.

Swim deeper into the ocean and explore the colourful coral reefs.

Open your eyes and take a deep breath in, feeling refreshed and full of wonder from our underwater adventure.

Mindful Eating: practice mindful eating exercises where children focus on the sensory experience of eating, paying attention to the taste, texture, and aroma of their food.

Movement and Body-Based Techniques

Yoga and Stretching:

Incorporate simple yoga poses and stretching exercises into the daily routine to help children release excess energy and improve attention span.

Dance and Movement:

Encourage children to engage in dance and movement activities to promote body awareness and sensory integration.

Grounding Stretches:

Introduce grounding stretches that emphasise connecting with the earth and feeling supported. For example, you can practice standing with your feet hip-width apart, rooting down through your feet, and reaching your arms overhead.

Breathwork with Movement:

Combine deep breathing exercises with gentle movement, such as swaying, rocking, or stretching. You can synchronise your breathing with movements, which will help regulate your nervous system and release tension.

Drumming Circles:

Facilitate drumming circles where individuals can engage in rhythmic drumming and percussion activities. Encourage them to focus on the beat of the drum and the vibration sensation in their body, helping them feel more grounded and connected to the group and to themselves.

By incorporating these tailored grounding techniques into the lives of children with learning difficulties, educators, therapists, and caregivers can provide essential support to help them thrive. Grounding techniques offer valuable tools for managing stress, regulating emotions, enhancing focus, and empowering children to navigate challenges with confidence and resilience. With consistent practice and support, children with learning difficulties can develop essential coping skills and build a foundation for success in school and beyond.

Grounding techniques that are tailored to children with learning difficulties' unique needs offer invaluable support in fostering emotional regulation, reducing anxiety, and enhancing overall well-being. By incorporating various sensory-based strategies, visual supports, auditory accommodations, movement activities, and mindfulness exercises, educators and caregivers can provide essential tools to help these children navigate their daily experiences with greater ease and confidence.

Whether it's engaging in sensory play, using visual schedules, practising deep breathing exercises, or incorporating movement breaks, these techniques empower children to connect with their bodies, minds, and environments in meaningful ways. Furthermore, grounding techniques promote a sense of empowerment and autonomy, allowing children to develop valuable coping skills and strategies for managing stress and adversity. By providing a supportive and inclusive environment that honours each child's unique strengths and challenges, educators and caregivers can create opportunities for growth, learning, and success.

It's important to recognise that every child is different, and what works for one may not work for another. Therefore, it's essential to approach grounding techniques with flexibility, patience, and compassion, tailoring interventions to meet each child's individual needs and preferences.

In essence, grounding techniques serve as powerful tools in the support toolkit for children with learning difficulties, empowering them to navigate the world's complexities with resilience, confidence, and a sense of belonging. Through ongoing collaboration, understanding, and advocacy, we can create environments where all children feel seen, valued, and capable of reaching their full potential.

Chapter 9: Grounding Techniques for Adults

Just as grounding techniques are tailored for the unique needs of children, adults, too, benefit immensely from practices that address the complexities of their lives. In this chapter, we explore a range of grounding techniques designed specifically for adults, acknowledging the diverse challenges they face in the realms of stress, emotional well-being, and the pursuit of mindfulness.

As adults navigate the intricate tapestry of life, marked by responsibilities, challenges, and the pursuit of balance, grounding techniques become invaluable tools for maintaining mental and emotional well-being. Tailored to address the unique complexities of adulthood, these techniques offer a sanctuary amidst the hustle and bustle of everyday life. This chapter delves into a range of grounding practices designed to empower adults to manage stress, cultivate emotional resilience, and foster mindfulness.

In the labyrinth of adult responsibilities, these grounding techniques serve as anchors, providing moments of solace and clarity. Incorporating these practices into daily routines empowers adults to navigate the complexities of life with resilience, mindfulness, and a profound sense of well-being. Just as children benefit from grounding techniques tailored to their needs, adults thrive when equipped with tools that resonate with the challenges and aspirations of their unique journey.

1. Deep Breathing Exercises for Stress Relief:

In the hustle and bustle of adult life, stress is a constant companion. Deep breathing exercises provide a powerful antidote, offering a moment of respite amidst the chaos. Techniques such as diaphragmatic breathing and box breathing become invaluable tools for adults, helping to alleviate stress, enhance focus, and promote a sense of calm. Deep breathing exercises are an effective way to reduce stress and promote relaxation.

Nadi Shodhana (Alternate Nostril Breathing):

Sit in a comfortable position with your spine straight and your left hand resting on your left knee.

Use your right thumb to close your right nostril and inhale deeply through your left nostril for a count of 4 seconds.

Close your left nostril with your right ring finger and hold your breath for a count of 4 seconds.

Release your right nostril and exhale slowly and completely for a count of 4 seconds.

Inhale deeply through your right nostril for a count of 4 seconds, close your right nostril, hold, and then exhale through your left nostril.

Repeat this cycle for several rounds, focusing on the smooth flow of breath through each nostril.

Practice deep breathing exercises regularly, especially during times of stress or tension, to promote relaxation, reduce anxiety, and improve overall well-being.

Diaphragmatic breathing:

Diaphragmatic breathing, also known as belly breathing or deep breathing, is a breathing technique that involves the contraction and relaxation of the diaphragm, a dome-shaped muscle located below the lungs. When you breathe in deeply, the diaphragm contracts and moves downward, allowing the lungs to expand fully and fill with air. This results in the abdomen (belly) expanding outward. When you exhale, the diaphragm relaxes and moves upward, pushing air out of the lungs.

Diaphragmatic breathing is characterised by the expansion of the abdomen rather than the chest during inhalation. It is considered a more efficient and relaxed way of breathing compared to shallow breathing, which primarily involves chest movement.

Practising diaphragmatic breathing has numerous benefits, including:

1. Promoting relaxation and reducing stress.

2. Increasing oxygen intake and improving lung function.

3. Lowering heart rate and blood pressure.

4. Enhancing focus, concentration, and mental clarity.

5. Stimulating the parasympathetic nervous system helps counteract the body's stress response.

Diaphragmatic breathing can be practised lying down, sitting, or standing. It's often used in relaxation techniques, meditation, yoga, and as a coping strategy for managing anxiety and stress. Learning to incorporate diaphragmatic breathing into your daily routine can contribute to your overall well-being and improve your physical and mental health.

To perform diaphragmatic breathing, follow these steps:

1. Find a Comfortable Position:

Sit or lie down in a comfortable position. You can choose to sit in a chair with your feet flat on the floor or lie down on your back with your knees bent and your feet flat on the bed or floor.

2. Relax Your Body:

Close your eyes and take a few deep breaths to relax your body and mind. Release any tension in your muscles, starting from your head and neck and working your way down to your toes.

3. Place Your Hands:

Place one hand on your chest and the other hand on your abdomen (just below your ribcage) to feel the movement of your breath.

4. Inhale Deeply:

Take a slow, deep breath in through your nose. As you inhale, focus on expanding your abdomen, allowing it to rise and push your hand outward. Try to keep your chest relatively still while your abdomen expands.

5. Exhale Slowly:

Gently exhale through your mouth, allowing your abdomen to fall inward as you release the air from your lungs. Feel the gentle contraction of your diaphragm as you exhale.

6. Repeat:

Continue to inhale deeply through your nose, expanding your abdomen, and exhale slowly through your mouth, allowing your abdomen to fall. Aim for a slow, steady rhythm of breathing.

7. Practice Regularly:

Practice diaphragmatic breathing for several minutes, gradually increasing the duration as you become more comfortable with the technique. You can incorporate it into your daily routine, such as before bedtime or during moments of stress or anxiety.

Remember to breathe comfortably and avoid forcing your breath. With practice, diaphragmatic breathing will become more natural, and you'll be able to use it as a tool to promote relaxation, reduce stress, and enhance overall well-being.

2. Mindful Meditation for Adults:

Meditation is a cornerstone of grounding for adults, offering a refuge from the demands of daily life. From mindful breathing to body scan meditations, these practices foster self-awareness, reduce anxiety, and enhance overall mental well-being.

Mindful meditation:

Settle into a Comfortable Position: Find a quiet and comfortable space where you can sit or lie down without distractions. Close your eyes gently or soften your gaze.

Focus on Your Breath:

Bring your attention to your breath. Notice the sensations of the breath as it enters and leaves your body. You can focus on the rising and falling of your chest, the sensation of air passing through your nostrils, or your abdomen's gentle expansion and contraction.

Observe Your Thoughts:

As you focus on your breath, thoughts may arise in your mind. Instead of getting caught up in or trying to suppress them, observe them without judgment. Allow your thoughts to come and go like clouds passing through the sky, gently bringing your attention back to your breath whenever you find yourself becoming distracted.

Return to the Present Moment:

When you notice your mind wandering or becoming distracted, gently redirect your attention to your breath. Use your breath as an anchor to the present moment, allowing it to guide you back whenever your thoughts begin to drift. Continue this practice for a few minutes, gradually lengthening the duration as you become more comfortable with the practice.

By practising this mindful meditation regularly, you can cultivate greater awareness, presence, and inner peace in your daily life.

3. Body Scan Meditation:

The body holds the key to understanding our emotional and physical states. Body scan meditation becomes a practice of turning inward, systematically bringing awareness to different parts of the body. This technique promotes relaxation, releases tension, and encourages a profound connection between mind and body.

Body scan meditation is a mindfulness practice that systematically brings awareness to different body parts, from head to toe, in a relaxed and non-judgmental way. Here's how to do a body scan meditation:

1. Find a Comfortable Position:

Sit or lie down in a comfortable position, with your back straight and your arms resting comfortably at your sides. Close your eyes if you feel comfortable doing so.

2. Begin with Deep Breaths:

Take a few deep breaths to relax your body and mind. Inhale deeply through your nose, filling your lungs with air, and exhale slowly through your mouth, releasing any tension or tightness in your body.

3. Bring Awareness to Your Body: Start by bringing your awareness to your feet. Notice any sensations you feel in your feet, such as warmth, tingling, or pressure. Allow your attention to rest on your feet for a few moments.

4. Move Upwards: Slowly move your awareness upward, bringing attention to each part of your body in turn. Notice the sensations in your legs, hips, abdomen, chest, back, shoulders, arms, hands, neck, and head. Take your time with each part of the body, allowing yourself to fully experience any sensations that arise.

5. Notice Without Judgment: As you scan each part of your body, try to observe any sensations with an attitude of curiosity and acceptance. Notice any tension or discomfort areas without judging or trying to change them. Simply observe and allow whatever is present to be.

6. Stay Present: If your mind starts to wander or you become distracted, gently bring your attention back to the present moment and continue with the body scan. You can use your breath as an anchor to help you stay focused.

7. End with Gratitude: Once you have scanned your entire body, take a moment to express gratitude for your body and all that it does for you. Notice how you feel physically, mentally, and emotionally after completing the body scan meditation.

Body scan meditation can help promote relaxation, reduce stress, and increase body awareness. It's a valuable practice for cultivating mindfulness and connecting with the present moment. Practice regularly to experience the benefits of this soothing meditation technique.

4. Yoga and Stretching as Grounding Activities:

Physical movement is a potent form of grounding. Yoga and stretching exercises catered to adults become a means of cultivating both physical and mental flexibility. These activities not only alleviate physical tension but also foster a sense of balance, strength, and mindfulness.

Adho Mukha Svanasana (Downward Facing Dog):

Start on your hands and knees, then lift your hips up and back, straightening your arms and legs to form an inverted V shape. Press your heels toward the ground and lengthen through your spine to stretch the back, hamstrings, calves, and shoulders.

Eka Pada Rajakapotasana (Pigeon Pose):

Start in a tabletop position, then bring your right knee forward toward your right wrist and your right foot toward your left wrist. Extend your left leg behind you, keeping your hips square, and fold forward over your front leg. Repeat on the other side. This pose stretches the hips and thighs.

Paschimottanasana (Seated Forward Fold):

Sit on the floor with your legs extended in front of you. Inhale to lengthen your spine, then exhale as you fold forward from your hips, reaching for your feet or shins. Keep your back straight and your chest open as you stretch the hamstrings and lower back.

5. Journaling and Self-Reflection:

The written word becomes a tool for self-discovery and emotional release. Journaling prompts and self-reflection exercises guide adults in exploring their thoughts and emotions, providing a structured outlet for processing experiences and fostering a deeper understanding of oneself.

In this chapter, we acknowledge that grounding for adults is a multifaceted journey encompassing various aspects of well-being. Whether through breath, meditation, movement, or introspection, adults can tap into a reservoir of techniques to navigate the complexities of their lives. Grounding becomes a personal sanctuary—a space for self-care, resilience, and the cultivation of a mindful and purposeful existence.

As we explore these techniques, remember that grounding is not a one-time fix but an ongoing practice. By incorporating these methods into daily life, adults can cultivate a resilient foundation that empowers them to face challenges with grace, embrace moments of joy, and navigate the ebb and flow of life with a sense of centeredness.

Chapter 10. How to use affirmations in grounding work

Affirmations play a pivotal role in grounding work, serving as powerful tools to foster a sense of stability, security, and inner peace. In the realm of mental health and emotional well-being, affirmations act as guiding lights, illuminating the path towards self-awareness and empowerment. By incorporating affirmations into grounding practices, individuals can cultivate a deeper connection to themselves and their surroundings, anchoring themselves firmly in the present moment.

Affirmations serve to challenge negative thought patterns and beliefs, replacing them with positive, uplifting messages that resonate with one's inner truth. For example, say, "I am grounded and present", or "I am connected to the earth's energy", or "I am rooted and grounded like a strong tree." Through repetition and intention, affirmations can reshape the landscape of the mind, fostering a more nurturing and compassionate internal dialogue. In grounding work, affirmations act as steady companions, offering reassurance and support during times of uncertainty or distress.

Moreover, affirmations have the remarkable ability to align thoughts, emotions, and actions, creating a harmonious synergy within the individual. By affirming statements that affirm one's strengths, values, and aspirations, individuals can cultivate a sense of self-confidence and resilience. Affirmations serve as reminders of one's inherent worth and potential, guiding them towards a path of growth, healing, and self-actualisation.

For children:

1. Keep it Simple: Word affirmations using language appropriate for their age. For example, "I am strong like a superhero."

2. Make it Fun: Incorporate playfulness into the affirmations to engage their imagination.

3. Visual Aids: Use visuals like drawings or posters with affirmations to make the grounding process more tangible.

For adults:

1. Tailor to Personal Needs: Create affirmations that address specific concerns or stressors individuals may be experiencing.

2. Incorporate Mindfulness: Combine affirmations with mindful breathing to enhance the grounding experience.

3. Regular Practice: Encourage consistent use of affirmations, integrating them into daily routines for ongoing support.

Affirmations are used in grounding work for several reasons because they can have a positive impact on mental, emotional, and physical well-being. Below are some of the key reasons why affirmations are beneficial in grounding practices:

1. Present Moment Affirmations:
Affirmations bring attention to the present moment, fostering mindfulness. By repeating positive statements, individuals become more aware of their thoughts and feelings, grounding themselves in the here and now.

2. Shifting Focus:

Affirmations help redirect attention from negative or anxious thoughts to more positive and empowering ones. This shift in focus can contribute to a sense of stability and control.

3. Building Positive Neural Pathways:

Repetition of affirmations can contribute to the formation of positive neural pathways in the brain. Over time, this can influence thought patterns and contribute to a more positive mindset.

4. Enhancing Emotional Well-being:

Affirmations are designed to evoke positive emotions. By consistently using affirmations, individuals can cultivate feelings of calmness, confidence, and gratitude, contributing to emotional well-being.

5. Encouraging Self-Compassion:

Affirmations often involve self-compassionate and encouraging language. This can be particularly helpful in grounding work and fostering a sense of self-love and acceptance.

6. Providing Stability in Uncertain Times:

Grounding work is often used during moments of stress, anxiety, or uncertainty. Affirmations offer a stable anchor, providing a sense of security and control in challenging situations.

7. Increasing Self-Awareness:

Affirmations can prompt individuals to reflect on their values, priorities, and strengths. This self-awareness is a critical component of grounding work, helping individuals connect with their authentic selves.

8. Encouraging Positive Behaviour:

Affirmations are not just about thoughts; they can influence actions. By reinforcing positive beliefs, individuals may be more inclined to engage in behaviours that align with those affirmations.

9. Cultivating a Positive Mindset:

Affirmations contribute to the cultivation of a positive mindset. When faced with challenges, individuals who regularly practice affirmations may be more likely to approach difficulties with a constructive and optimistic outlook.

10. Supporting Overall Well-being:

Grounding work aims to support holistic well-being, encompassing mental, emotional, and physical health. Affirmations play a role in this by addressing the cognitive and emotional aspects of an individual's experience.

In essence, affirmations serve as potent catalysts for transformation in grounding work, fostering a more profound sense of presence, purpose, and authenticity. By integrating affirmations into daily practice, individuals can cultivate a solid foundation upon which to navigate life's challenges with grace and resilience.

Chapter 11: Incorporating Nature into Grounding

In the tapestry of grounding techniques, the embrace of nature emerges as a powerful thread, weaving through the fabric of well-being for children and adults. This chapter explores the therapeutic benefits of connecting with the natural world, offering a sanctuary where the mind can find peace, the senses can awaken, and the spirit can rejuvenate.

In the symphony of grounding techniques, the harmony of nature provides a timeless melody that resonates with children and adults. The therapeutic benefits of connecting with the natural world extend beyond mere moments of tranquillity; they encompass a holistic rejuvenation of the mind, body, and spirit.

In the embrace of nature, grounding transcends the ordinary; it becomes a journey of reconnection with the earth, a dance with the elements, and a rejuvenation of the soul. As both children and adults can integrate the therapeutic benefits of nature into their grounding practices, they find not only solace but also a profound sense of belonging to the intricate web of life. Nature, in its myriad forms, becomes a timeless sanctuary where the mind finds peace, the senses awaken, and the spirit is revitalised.

1. Nature's Calming Effect:

Nature has an inherent ability to soothe the soul. Understanding the symbiotic relationship between humans and nature provides the foundation for incorporating the outdoors into grounding practices.

2. Outdoor Grounding Activities for Both Children and Adults:

Step outside and immerse yourself in the healing embrace of the natural world. You can explore various outdoor grounding activities suitable for children and adults. From mindful walks and nature scavenger hunts to simply sitting and absorbing sights and sounds, these activities harness the therapeutic power of nature to promote mindfulness and inner peace.

3. The Therapeutic Benefits of Spending Time in Natural Surroundings:

Explore the profound therapeutic benefits of spending time in natural surroundings. From stress reduction and improved mood to increased creativity and enhanced well-being, you can uncover the transformative impact that nature can have on mental and emotional health.

4. Connecting with Nature Through Walks, Hikes, or Gardening:

Whether it's a leisurely stroll, an invigorating hike, or tending to a garden, a physical connection with nature becomes a source of grounding. Engaging the senses in these activities fosters mindfulness, encourages a sense of presence, and provides a tangible link to the cycles of life.

Engaging with nature through walks, hikes, or gardening is a wonderful way to connect with the natural world, reduce stress, and promote overall well-being. Here's how to enjoy nature through these activities:

Nature Walks:

Find a nearby park, nature reserve, or trail where you can go for a leisurely walk. Take your time to observe the sights, sounds, and smells of nature around you.

Notice the colours of the trees and flowers, the songs of the birds, and the feel of the sun on your skin. Allow yourself to be fully present in the moment and appreciate the beauty of your surroundings.

Take deep breaths of fresh air and feel the sensation of walking on the earth beneath your feet. Use this time to clear your mind, reduce stress, and recharge your energy.

Hiking Adventures:

Explore hiking trails in your area that offer varying levels of difficulty and terrain. Choose a trail that suits your fitness level and interests, whether a gentle nature walk or a more challenging hike.

Bring along water, snacks, and appropriate gear, such as sturdy shoes and clothing layers. Take breaks along the way to rest, hydrate, and enjoy the scenery.

Challenge yourself to reach a scenic overlook, waterfall, or summit, and reward yourself with breathtaking views and a sense of accomplishment.

Gardening Activities:

Create a garden space in your backyard, balcony, or windowsill where you can grow flowers, herbs, vegetables or a pot plant. Get your hands dirty as you plant seeds, water plants, and tend to your garden.

Pay attention to the needs of your plants and observe their growth and development over time. Cultivate a sense of patience, nurturing, and connection with the natural world.

Take moments to simply sit and enjoy your garden, listening to the sounds of birds chirping and bees buzzing. Notice the beauty of the flowers in bloom and the tranquillity of the greenery surrounding you.

Whether you're going for a nature walk, embarking on a hiking adventure, or tending to your garden, spending time in nature can have numerous benefits for your physical, mental, and emotional well-being. Enjoy the opportunity to reconnect with the natural world and nourish your soul with its beauty and vitality.

In this chapter, nature becomes more than just a backdrop; it becomes an active participant in the grounding journey. Children and adults tap into a wellspring of resilience, balance, and inspiration by cultivating a mindful connection with the natural world. Nature becomes a teacher, offering valuable lessons in all living things' presence, adaptability, and interconnectedness.

As you explore the marriage of grounding techniques with the great outdoors, remember that nature is not a distant destination—it is a living, breathing companion on your journey to well-being. Whether under the open sky, among the trees, or in the simple act of tending to a garden, nature becomes a sanctuary where the spirit finds solace, the mind finds clarity, and the heart finds peace.

Chapter 12: Grounding in Daily Life

Grounding is not reserved for special moments or circumstances—it is a practice woven into the fabric of our daily lives. In this chapter, we explore how grounding techniques can seamlessly integrate into everyday routines, becoming a natural and accessible part of children's and adults' lives. By incorporating grounding into daily life, we transform it from a mere activity into a way of being.

1. Integrating Grounding Techniques into Everyday Routines:

Discover the art of infusing grounding techniques into the rhythm of daily life. Simple practices, such as mindful breathing during daily commutes, incorporating moments of stillness into morning routines, or using sensory exploration during breaks, can seamlessly integrate grounding into the flow of the day.

2. Creating a Grounding Toolkit for Easy Access:

Build a personalised grounding toolkit that aligns with your preferences and lifestyle. You can create a toolkit that includes quick grounding exercises, visual reminders, and sensory tools. This toolkit becomes an easily accessible resource, ready to provide support whenever stressors arise.

3. Identifying Personal Triggers and Using Grounding Techniques Proactively:

Understanding personal triggers is a crucial aspect of proactive grounding. Individuals can navigate daily life with greater resilience by staying ahead of challenges to maintain emotional equilibrium.

4. Encouraging a Supportive Environment for Grounding:

Fostering a supportive environment is essential for successful grounding. It is important that families, schools, and workplaces can encourage and integrate grounding practices. By creating spaces prioritising well-being, individuals of all ages can feel empowered to incorporate grounding techniques into their daily routines.

Encouraging and integrating grounding practices into families, schools, and workplaces can significantly benefit individuals by promoting well-being, reducing stress, and fostering a sense of connection.

Families:

1. Lead by Example:

Parents and caregivers can model grounding practices by incorporating them into their own daily routines. Children are more likely to adopt these practices if they see adults engaging in them regularly.

2. Create a Calm Environment:

Establish a peaceful and nurturing home environment that supports grounding practices. This can include creating designated quiet spaces for meditation or relaxation, minimising screen time, and prioritising time outdoors in nature.

3. Practice Mindful Communication:

Encourage open and honest communication within the family and teach children how to express their thoughts and emotions in a mindful way. Use techniques such as active listening and empathy to foster connection and understanding.

4. Establish Family Rituals:

Incorporate grounding practices into family rituals and routines. This could include beginning or ending the day with a family mindfulness practice, sharing gratitude during meals, or going for nature walks together on weekends.

Schools:

1. Integrate Mindfulness into the Curriculum:

Incorporate mindfulness and grounding practices into the school curriculum through activities, exercises, and lessons. This could include daily mindfulness activities before and at the end of the lesson for 5 minutes, mindful breathing exercises before tests or exams, or incorporating nature-based learning experiences into the curriculum and recognising when children are struggling and giving them an opportunity to do a grounding activity such as breathing or visualisation activity.

2. Create Mindful Spaces:

Designate areas within the school environment where students and staff can engage in mindfulness and grounding practices. This could be a quiet corner with cushions and meditation tools, an outdoor garden or green space, or a sensory room equipped with calming sensory materials.

3. Encourage Peer Support:

Foster a sense of community and peer support by encouraging students to engage in grounding practices together. This could include buddy systems for mindfulness activities, peer-led meditation groups, or collaborative nature-based projects.

Workplaces:

1. Promote Work-Life Balance:

Encourage employees to prioritise their well-being by promoting work-life balance and offering flexible scheduling options. Provide opportunities for employees to take breaks, recharge, and engage in grounding practices throughout the workday.

2. Offer Mindfulness Programs:

Implement mindfulness programs or initiatives in the workplace, such as lunchtime meditation sessions, mindfulness workshops, or wellness challenges focused on grounding practices. Provide resources and support for employees to develop their mindfulness skills.

3. Create Zen Spaces:

Designate quiet areas within the workplace where employees can go to unwind, relax, and practice mindfulness. This could be a designated meditation room, a green space with plants and natural light, or a cosy lounge area with comfortable seating.

4. Encourage Mindful Leadership:

Foster a culture of mindful leadership by encouraging managers and supervisors to lead by example and prioritise their own well-being. Provide leadership training and support for managers to develop their mindfulness skills and integrate grounding practices into their leadership style.

By implementing these strategies, families, schools, and workplaces can create environments that support and encourage grounding practices, leading to greater well-being, resilience, and connection for individuals of all ages.

In this chapter, grounding transcends the role of a standalone practice and becomes a guiding philosophy for living intentionally. Through the seamless integration of grounding techniques into daily life, children and adults alike cultivate a sense of presence, resilience, and emotional balance. Grounding becomes a companion, accompanying individuals through the ebb and flow of their daily experiences.

As you explore the practical application of grounding in daily life, remember that these techniques are not meant to add complexity but rather to simplify and enhance your everyday experiences. Grounding, therefore, becomes a gentle yet profound undercurrent, supporting you as you navigate the complexities of modern living with mindfulness, purpose, and a centred heart.

Chapter 13: Tailoring Grounding Techniques for Specific Needs

Recognising that individuals have unique experiences and challenges, this chapter delves into the art of tailoring grounding techniques to specific needs. Whether addressing anxiety, stress, anger or focusing on trauma recovery, grounding practices can be adapted to provide targeted support for both children and adults.

In the diverse landscape of human experiences, recognising and responding to individual needs is crucial when it comes to grounding techniques. This chapter delves into the nuanced art of tailoring these practices to address specific challenges, acknowledging that one size does not fit all. Whether the focus is on anxiety, stress, anger management, or trauma recovery, understanding how to adapt grounding techniques offers a personalised approach that can be profoundly transformative for both children and adults.

In essence, tailoring grounding techniques to specific needs is an art that involves a deep understanding of individual experiences. By customising these practices, we acknowledge the unique challenges individuals face and provide them with tools that resonate with their journey toward well-being. Whether it's managing anxiety, navigating trauma, or addressing specific conditions, a personalised approach to grounding techniques can be a guiding light on the path to healing and resilience.

1. Anxiety Relief:

Tailoring Mindful Breathing and Visualization: For individuals grappling with anxiety, techniques that emphasise slow, intentional breathing and guided visualisation can be particularly effective. Personalising a mental sanctuary through visualisation provides a calming refuge during anxious moments. Using imagery that the child or adult feels comfortable with is key to personalising guided visualisation techniques. If the child or adult is interested in trains or going to the beach, incorporating these interests will facilitate the child or adult to connect to the guided visualisation.

2. Stress Management:

Progressive Muscle Relaxation (PMR): Tailoring grounding techniques for stress management often involves physical relaxation. With its systematic tension and release approach, PMR is a powerful tool for dissipating stress and promoting a sense of calm.

3. Anger Control:

Grounding through Sensory Distraction: Engaging the senses can redirect intense emotions when dealing with anger. Encouraging individuals to focus on sensory experiences—touching a textured object, listening to calming music, or taking a walk—provides a constructive outlet for anger.

4. Trauma Recovery:

Trauma-Informed Grounding Practices: Individuals on the path of trauma recovery require special consideration. Grounding techniques need to be approached with sensitivity, incorporating trauma-informed practices such as anchoring exercises, safety affirmations, and gradual exposure to grounding activities.

Trauma-informed grounding practices are essential tools for individuals who have experienced trauma, as they provide a means to regulate overwhelming emotions, reduce anxiety, and establish a sense of safety and stability. These practices focus on reconnecting individuals with the present moment and their bodies, helping them feel grounded and anchored amidst distressing thoughts and sensations. Additionally, trauma-informed approaches emphasise the importance of creating a safe and supportive environment where individuals feel empowered to engage in grounding practices at their own pace and with respect to their boundaries. By incorporating trauma-informed grounding practices into therapeutic interventions, individuals can learn effective coping strategies, increase resilience, and embark on a path toward healing and recovery.

There are essential techniques which are trauma-informed grounding practices that are used in therapy and mental health support to help individuals manage distressing emotions, reduce anxiety, and establish a sense of safety and stability. These practices recognise the impact of trauma on the body and mind and aim to provide tools for individuals to regulate their nervous system and reconnect with the present moment.

5. Grief and Loss:

Nature-Based Reflection: Grounding techniques for individuals coping with grief often involve connecting with nature. Reflective practices in natural settings, such as memorial walks or creating a memorial garden, provide a gentle yet powerful way to navigate the complexities of loss.

6. Depression:

Expressive Arts and Journaling: Individuals dealing with depression can find solace in expressive arts and journaling. Encouraging creative outlets, such as painting, writing, or engaging in other artistic pursuits, serves as a therapeutic means of self-expression.

Visual Arts:

Express your feelings through drawing, painting, or collage. Use a variety of art materials and create without judgment or expectation. Art can serve as a non-verbal way to communicate difficult emotions and provide a sense of release and catharsis.

Music as Therapy:

Use music as a tool for emotional expression and connection. Listen to or create music that resonates with your mood and experiences. Music can evoke powerful emotions and provide comfort and solace during times of distress.

7. Performance Anxiety:

Tailoring grounding techniques for performance anxiety often involves building confidence through positive affirmations and visualisation. Guiding individuals to visualise successful outcomes and reinforcing positive self-talk can alleviate performance-related stress.

Positive Affirmations for Performance Anxiety for Children:

"I am brave and capable of doing my best. I trust myself to handle whatever comes my way, and I am proud of my efforts, no matter the outcome."

"I am unique and special just the way I am. I am confident in my abilities, and I believe in myself. I can overcome challenges and shine bright."

Positive Affirmations for Performance Anxiety for Adults:

"I am calm, confident, and fully prepared for this moment. I trust in my abilities and embrace the opportunity to showcase my talents with ease and grace."

"I am worthy of success and capable of achieving my goals. I approach challenges with courage and determination, knowing that each experience strengthens my resilience and expands my potential."

These affirmations are designed to instil confidence, self-belief, and a sense of readiness in individuals facing performance anxiety. They can be repeated regularly, particularly before and during stressful situations, reinforcing positive thoughts and attitudes.

8. Sleep Disturbances:

Grounding techniques for promoting restful sleep include establishing relaxation rituals before bedtime. Incorporating calming activities such as warm baths, gentle stretches, or guided relaxation exercises helps create a conducive environment for sleep.

9. Addressing Anxiety and Stress:

Anxiety and stress are prevalent in the fast-paced world we live in. From quick, on-the-go exercises for immediate relief to more immersive practices for long-term stress management, individuals can learn how to ground themselves amidst the whirlwind of anxious thoughts and stressors.

Physical Activity:

Incorporate regular exercise into your routine to release endorphins, improve mood, and reduce symptoms of anxiety and stress.

Healthy Lifestyle Habits:

Maintain a balanced diet, prioritise adequate sleep, and limit caffeine and alcohol consumption to support overall well-being and stress management.

Time Management:

Organise your schedule and prioritise tasks to reduce feelings of overwhelm and improve productivity.

Set Boundaries:

Establish healthy boundaries in your relationships and commitments to prevent burnout and protect your mental and emotional well-being.

10. Grounding Techniques for Anger Management:

Anger is a natural emotion, but learning how to manage it constructively is crucial. Techniques such as breathwork, mindfulness exercises, and physical activities become tools to navigate the turbulent waters of anger, fostering emotional regulation and self-control.

Self-Talk:

Use self-talk to challenge negative thoughts, reinforce self-control and relieve your Anger. Remind yourself of your strengths, values, and goals, and encourage yourself to make thoughtful decisions.

Create a Plan:

Develop a proactive plan for managing challenging situations and triggers. Identify potential triggers in advance and brainstorm coping strategies to help you stay grounded, maintain self-control, and relieve your Anger.

11. Techniques for Improving Focus and Attention:

Maintaining focus and attention can be challenging in a world full of distractions. From sensory-focused activities to mindfulness meditation, individuals of all ages can discover methods to sharpen their focus and engage more fully in the present moment.

Chunking:

Break down tasks into smaller, manageable chunks to prevent overwhelm and facilitate focus. Focus on one task or subtask at a time, and reward yourself for each accomplishment to maintain momentum.

Time Blocking:

Allocate specific blocks of time for focused work and minimise distractions during these periods. Use timers or productivity apps to track your progress and maintain accountability.

Physical Movement:

Incorporate brief physical movements or stretches into your routine to rejuvenate your body and mind. Take short breaks to walk around, stretch, or do a quick exercise to re-energize and refocus.

12. Grounding for Trauma Recovery:

Trauma can leave a lasting impact on mental and emotional well-being. Techniques are tailored to provide a safe and supportive space for individuals to reconnect with their bodies, build resilience, and gradually navigate the path toward healing.

Seeking support from a qualified mental health therapist is often needed in trauma recovery as the individual will need personalised support related to the individual's trauma. The use of grounding techniques is a cornerstone in trauma recovery.

In this chapter, grounding techniques become personalised tools for empowerment and healing. By tailoring practices to specific needs, children and adults can address challenges with intentionality and self-compassion. Grounding is not a one-size-fits-all solution; it is a flexible and adaptive practice that evolves alongside the unique needs of individuals on their journey to well-being.

As we explore the tailored application of grounding techniques, remember that customisation is a strength. Embrace the opportunity to discover what works best for you or for those you support. Grounding becomes a personalised roadmap, guiding individuals toward emotional balance, resilience, and a profound sense of self-awareness.

Chapter 14: Practicing Mindfulness in Relationships

In the intricate dance of human connections, mindfulness emerges as a guiding force, enriching relationships and fostering more profound connections. This chapter explores how grounding techniques can be woven into the fabric of interpersonal dynamics, offering children and adults the tools to cultivate mindful communication, empathy, and supportive connections.

In the intricate dance of human connections, the practice of mindfulness serves as a transformative force, shaping the dynamics of relationships and fostering deeper, more meaningful connections. By delving into the integration of grounding techniques into the fabric of interpersonal relationships and cultivating mindfulness in communication, empathy, and overall connection, children and adults can embrace a more intentional and harmonious way of relating to one another.

In the realm of relationships, the practice of mindfulness through grounding techniques transforms the ordinary into the extraordinary. By intentionally weaving these practices into the tapestry of connection, children and adults can nurture relationships built on understanding, empathy, and shared moments of mindful presence. Grounding techniques become not only tools for personal well-being but also bridges that connect individuals, creating a harmonious dance of mindfulness in the beautiful complexity of human relationships.

1. Building Connection Through Mindful Communication:

Effective communication is the cornerstone of healthy relationships. Grounding techniques are harnessed to enhance mindful communication. By cultivating a space for open and non-judgmental dialogue that encourages active listening, thoughtful expression, and a deeper understanding of each other's perspectives, relationships become enriched and strengthened.

2. Sharing Grounding Techniques with Family and Friends:

Grounding is a journey that can be shared. It is important to introduce grounding techniques to family and friends. By creating a shared language of well-being, individuals can support one another in moments of stress, celebrate successes, and collectively weave a tapestry of mindfulness within their relationships.

Grounding becomes a collaborative effort, especially within families and close-knit communities. Techniques for recognising and responding to each other's needs foster a culture of mutual understanding, empathy, and shared well-being.

Sharing grounding techniques with family and friends can be immensely beneficial for promoting emotional well-being and fostering supportive relationships.

Lead by Example:

Incorporate grounding techniques into your own daily routine and openly discuss their benefits with your family and friends. Demonstrating how these techniques help you manage stress and stay centred can inspire others to try them out.

Start Small:

Introduce simple grounding techniques that are easy to understand and implement, such as deep breathing exercises, sensory grounding, or mindfulness practices. Encourage family members and friends to start with techniques that resonate with them.

Practice Together:

Set aside time to practice grounding techniques together as a group. This could involve doing a guided meditation, going for a nature walk, or engaging in a creative activity like drawing or journaling.

Create a Supportive Environment:

Foster an environment where everyone feels comfortable sharing their experiences with grounding techniques. Encourage open communication and provide support and encouragement as needed.

Be Patient:

Understand that it may take time for family members and friends to feel comfortable with grounding techniques and experience their benefits. Be patient and supportive throughout the process, and celebrate each other's progress.

Regular Check-Ins:

Schedule regular check-ins with family members and friends to discuss how they're incorporating grounding techniques into their lives and any challenges they may be facing. Offer encouragement and problem-solving support as needed.

In this chapter, mindfulness becomes a bridge connecting hearts and minds in relationships. Grounding techniques are not only individual practices but also tools for creating shared moments of presence, understanding, and connection. Whether in families, friendships, or partnerships, incorporating mindfulness elevates relationships to a space of mutual growth, support, and emotional intimacy.

As you explore the application of grounding techniques in relationships, remember that the journey of well-being is communal. Embrace the opportunity to weave mindfulness into the fabric of your connections, recognising that the practice of grounding not only transforms individual experiences but also enriches the collective tapestry of relationships in a shared commitment to presence and understanding.

Chapter 15: Overcoming Challenges in Practicing Grounding

Embarking on the journey of grounding is a transformative endeavour, promising a richer connection with oneself and the world. However, this path has its challenges. There are common obstacles that individuals, both children and adults, may encounter on their grounding journey.

In the face of challenges, the journey of grounding becomes an opportunity for growth and resilience. By acknowledging and addressing obstacles with patience, adaptability, and a personalised approach, individuals can overcome hurdles on their path to well-being. As a transformative practice, Grounding remains accessible and empowering, guiding individuals toward a more balanced and harmonious existence.

1. Resistance to Change:
Some individuals may resist incorporating grounding practices into their routine due to a fear of change. Gradual integration, starting with small and manageable practices, helps overcome resistance and allows for a more comfortable adjustment to grounding techniques.

2. Micro-Moments of Grounding:
In our fast-paced world, the perception of not having enough time is a common challenge. Encouraging individuals to incorporate micro-moments of grounding—short, intentional practices that can be done in a few minutes—ensures that the benefits of grounding can be realised even in the busiest of schedules.

3. Cultivating Patience:
Grounding is a gradual process, and individuals may become impatient with the pace of results. Cultivating patience and recognising that the benefits may unfold over time is essential. Regular reflection on progress can help reinforce the positive impact of grounding practices.

4. Adapting Techniques for Attention Difficulties:
Individuals with difficulty focusing may find engaging in specific grounding techniques challenging. Adapting practices to suit their needs, incorporating movement or sensory elements, can enhance focus and make grounding more accessible to all.

5. Exploring and Experiencing:
Some individuals may approach grounding with scepticism or doubt. Encouraging them to explore various techniques and experience the positive effects firsthand can help overcome scepticism. Personal anecdotes and testimonials from others who have benefited can also be persuasive.

6. Establishing Routine:
Inconsistency in practising grounding techniques can impede their effectiveness. Establishing a routine, incorporating grounding into daily habits, and setting reminders can help individuals stay committed to their practice.

7. Respecting Personal Beliefs:
Grounding practices may intersect with cultural or religious beliefs. It's crucial to respect and adapt techniques to align with individual values. Encouraging the exploration of grounding practices that are culturally or spiritually relevant can overcome such barriers.

8. Personalised Guidance:
The vast array of grounding techniques can be overwhelming. Offering personalised guidance, perhaps through consultations with professionals or self-discovery exercises, helps individuals identify techniques that resonate with them.

9. Trauma-Informed Approaches:
Individuals with a history of trauma may face specific challenges in grounding. Employing trauma-informed approaches, seeking professional guidance, and introducing gentle, non-triggering techniques can help navigate these challenges safely.

10. Creating Environmental Cues:
Integrating grounding into daily life requires intentional effort. Creating environmental cues, such as placing a grounding object in a visible area, can serve as reminders. Linking grounding practices to existing habits also aids in seamless integration.

11. Strategies for Overcoming Resistance:
Resistance to new practices is a natural part of change. Whether it's addressing scepticism, fear, or discomfort, individuals can learn how to navigate these hurdles and open themselves up to the potential benefits of grounding.

As we navigate the challenges inherent in grounding practices, it's crucial to recognise that the journey is unique for each individual. By acknowledging obstacles and implementing practical strategies, children and adults can cultivate a resilient mindset and overcome barriers on their path to a more grounded and balanced life.

In this chapter, we embrace the imperfections and triumphs of the grounding journey, recognising that challenges are stepping stones to growth. Grounding becomes not only a set of techniques but a testament to one's commitment to well-being. By addressing obstacles with intentionality and perseverance, individuals can navigate the bumps along the road, emerging more robust, grounded, and better equipped to face life's ever-changing landscape.

Chapter 16: Empowering Self-Care through Grounding

In the pursuit of well-being, self-care is a vital component that often takes a backseat in the hustle and bustle of life. This chapter explores the empowering intersection of grounding techniques and self-care, illustrating how these practices can be woven into daily life to foster resilience, emotional balance, and a profound sense of self-nurturing for children and adults.

In the relentless rhythm of modern life, self-care emerges as a beacon of well-being, yet the demands of daily existence frequently overshadow it. This chapter illuminates the empowering intersection of grounding techniques and self-care, showcasing how these practices can be seamlessly woven into everyday life to cultivate resilience, emotional balance, and a profound sense of self-nurturing for children and adults.

Individuals discover a reservoir of strength, resilience, and balance in the empowering intersection of grounding techniques and self-care. By infusing these practices into daily routines, children and adults can embark on a journey of self-nurturing, fostering emotional well-being, and creating a foundation for a life guided by intentional self-care. Grounding becomes not just a practice but a gateway to a harmonious and empowered existence.

1. Setting Intentions for the Day:
Infusing grounding techniques into morning rituals establishes a positive tone for the day. Mindful breathing, visualisation, or gentle stretches become acts of self-care, grounding individuals in a centred and intentional mindset.

2. Micro-Moments of Self-Care:
Incorporating grounding practices into short breaks throughout the day offers moments of rejuvenation. Whether it's a brief mindfulness exercise, a walk in nature, or a sensory grounding activity, these micro-moments become acts of self-care.

3. Evening Wind-Down:
As the day concludes, grounding techniques can facilitate a peaceful transition to the evening. Journaling, progressive muscle relaxation, or calming visualisation exercises create a serene wind-down routine, promoting restful sleep and emotional well-being.

4. Nature as a Self-Care Sanctuary:
Connecting with nature becomes a powerful form of self-care. Whether it's a mindful nature walk, gardening, or simply spending time outdoors, nature serves as a sanctuary for grounding, fostering a deep sense of connection and rejuvenation.

5. Savouring the Moment:
Grounding techniques can be integrated into meals, transforming the act of eating into a mindful experience. Paying attention to the sensory aspects of food, practising gratitude before meals, and savouring each bite contributes to nourishing the body and soul.

6. Digital Detox and Unplugging:
Grounding through a digital detox is a form of self-care in the digital age. Unplugging from screens and technology at designated times creates space for personal reflection, reducing information overload and promoting mental well-being.

7. Self-Compassion Practices:
Grounding techniques can be intertwined with self-compassion practices. Positive affirmations, self-appreciation exercises, and self-reflective grounding activities contribute to fostering a compassionate relationship with oneself.

8. Creative Expression:
Grounding practices can be channelled into creative expression. Engaging in art, writing, music, or any form of creative outlet becomes a medium for self-discovery, emotional release, and a celebration of individuality.

9. Mindful Movement for Physical Well-Being:
Grounding techniques extend into mindful movement practices. Activities like yoga, tai chi, or dance enhance physical well-being and cultivate mindfulness, creating a holistic approach to self-care.

10. Establishing Personal Boundaries:

Grounding techniques support the establishment of personal boundaries. Prioritising self-care and recognising the importance of emotional well-being contribute to a resilient and empowered sense of self.

11.   Celebrating Successes and Progress in Grounding Practices: Acknowledging and celebrating successes, no matter how small, is essential to sustaining a self-care routine. Individuals are motivated to continue their self-care journey with a sense of accomplishment by cultivating a positive and affirming mindset.

In this chapter, grounding practices become not just tools for managing stress but a celebration of one's commitment to personal well-being. By embracing self-care through grounding, both children and adults can navigate the complexities of life with intentionality, resilience, and a profound connection to their inner sanctuary of peace.

Chapter 17: Encouragement to make grounding a lifelong practice

Encouraging individuals to make grounding a lifelong practice involves highlighting the long-term benefits and emphasising the transformative impact it can have on their overall well-being. Here are some points to encourage the adoption of grounding as a lifelong practice:

1. A holistic approach to well-being:

Grounding is not just a temporary fix but a holistic approach to well-being. It addresses emotional, mental, and physical aspects of life, promoting a sense of balance that extends to various areas, including relationships, work, and personal growth.

2. Building Emotional Resilience:

Grounding techniques equip individuals with tools to navigate life's challenges with resilience. By fostering emotional regulation and coping skills, grounding becomes a lifelong companion, providing support during times of stress, uncertainty, and adversity.

3. Integrating Grounding into Daily Rituals:

Encourage the integration of grounding into daily habits. Making it a part of morning routines, work breaks, and evening wind-downs helps establish a consistent practice. Over time, these habits become second nature, contributing to a mindful and intentional way of living.

4. Stress Reduction and Emotional Well-Being:

There are several long-term mental health benefits of grounding, such as stress reduction, improved emotional regulation, and a positive impact on mood.

5. Grounding Across Life Stages:

Whether navigating the challenges of adolescence, the responsibilities of adulthood, or the transitions of later years, grounding remains a flexible and valuable tool.

6. A Tool for Continuous Self-Discovery:

As individuals evolve and face new experiences, grounding practices provide a constant anchor, supporting their journey of self-awareness and development.

7. Building Meaningful Connections:

By fostering empathy, active listening, and effective communication, individuals can cultivate meaningful relationships throughout their lives.

8. Incorporating Grounding into Lifestyle Choices:

As you make choices related to nutrition, physical activity, and self-care, grounding becomes a complementary element that enhances your overall health and well-being.

9. Investing in Preventive Mental Health:

Regular practice can contribute to a resilient mental health foundation, potentially reducing the risk of stress-related disorders and promoting long-term psychological well-being.

10. Passing Down Positive Habits:

By incorporating grounding into family routines, individuals not only benefit personally but also contribute to a culture of well-being within their families and communities.

By framing grounding as a lifelong practice with enduring benefits, individuals are more likely to embrace it as an integral part of their journey toward a balanced, mindful, and empowered life. It becomes not just a technique but a guiding philosophy that enriches their entire life story.

Chapter 18: The transformative power of staying grounded in a fast-paced world

In a fast-paced world, the transformative power of staying grounded is profound, offering individuals a means to navigate the whirlwind of modern life with resilience, balance, and a sense of inner peace. Here are critical aspects of the transformative power of staying grounded:

1. Cultivating Resilience:

Staying grounded provides a foundation for resilience. Individuals equipped with grounding techniques can face challenges with a centred mindset, adapting to changes and setbacks more effectively.

2. Emotional Regulation:

Grounding acts as a stabilising force for emotions. In a fast-paced world where stress is prevalent, staying grounded helps individuals regulate their emotions, reducing the impact of external pressures on their mental well-being.

3. Mindful Decision-Making:

Grounding fosters mindfulness, enabling individuals to make decisions with clarity and intention. In a fast-paced environment, the ability to pause, reflect, and make thoughtful choices becomes a transformative power that can shape one's path.

4. Reducing Anxiety and Stress:

Staying grounded is a potent antidote to anxiety and stress. Grounding techniques, such as deep breathing or mindfulness exercises, offer moments of calm amidst the chaos, preventing the accumulation of stressors.

5. Improved Focus and Productivity:

Grounding practices contribute to improved focus and cognitive performance. In a world filled with distractions, staying grounded helps individuals concentrate on tasks, boosting productivity and efficiency.

6. Connecting with the Present Moment:

Grounding encourages individuals to connect with the present moment. This transformative shift from the constant rush of the future or dwelling on the past fosters a deeper appreciation for the "now."

7. Healthy Work-Life Balance:

Staying grounded empowers individuals to set boundaries and prioritise well-being. In a world that often blurs the lines between work and personal life, grounding becomes a transformative force in establishing a healthy balance.

8. Promoting Physical Well-Being:

Grounding techniques, including movement-based practices like yoga or tai chi, contribute to physical well-being. They alleviate tension, improve posture, and enhance overall bodily health.

9. Enhanced Interpersonal Connections:

Staying grounded positively impacts interpersonal connections. Grounded individuals bring a centred and empathetic presence to their relationships, fostering deeper connections with others.

10. Increased Self-Awareness:

Grounding initiates a journey of self-awareness. In a world that often pushes individuals to conform, staying grounded allows for authentic self-discovery, leading to personal growth and fulfilment.

11. Spiritual and Transcendent Experiences:

Some grounding practices, such as mindfulness or nature connection, can lead to spiritual and transcendent experiences. Staying grounded opens the door to a deeper connection with oneself and the universe.

12. A Source of Stability:

Staying grounded is akin to creating an inner sanctuary. In a rapidly changing world, this sanctuary serves as a stable anchor, providing individuals with a sense of security and peace amid external uncertainties.

13. Encouraging a Sustainable Lifestyle:

Grounding often extends to fostering an awareness of sustainable living. Individuals who stay grounded are more likely to make environmentally conscious choices, contributing to a healthier planet.

14. Embracing the Journey, Not Just the Destination:

Grounding encourages individuals to embrace the journey rather than fixate solely on goals. In a world obsessed with achievement, staying grounded fosters an appreciation for the present and the joy found in each step of the journey.

15. Personal Empowerment:

Staying grounded empowers individuals to take control of their responses amid chaos. This transformative power lies in the ability to navigate life with a sense of agency and a grounded perspective.

In the fast-paced currents of the modern world, staying grounded becomes a transformative practice that shields individuals from the storm and empowers them to dance with the rhythm of life with grace and resilience. It is an inward journey that radiates outward, transforming not only the individual but also the world they engage with.

Chapter 19: Setting Intentions

In the realm of grounding techniques, setting intentions serves as the cornerstone upon which the journey towards inner peace and stability begins. Whether it is a children or adults, the act of setting intentions provides a roadmap for navigating the complexities of the mind and emotions.

Understanding Intentions:

Intentions are more than just fleeting thoughts or desires; they are deliberate statements of purpose that guide our actions and shape our experiences. When we set intentions, we are declaring our commitment to a particular outcome or state of being. In the context of grounding, intentions serve as anchors that tether us to the present moment and help us cultivate a sense of inner balance and clarity.

The Importance of Clarity:

Before embarking on any grounding practice, it's essential to cultivate clarity of intention. This clarity enables us to align our thoughts, emotions, and actions with our overarching goals and values. Whether cultivating a sense of calm, finding clarity amidst chaos, or fostering self-compassion, the clarity of intention provides a clear focal point for our grounding journey.

Crafting Meaningful Intentions:

Crafting meaningful intentions requires a deep exploration of our inner landscape and a willingness to confront our fears, insecurities, and limitations. Rather than focusing solely on external outcomes, meaningful intentions delve into the essence of who we are and who we aspire to become. They reflect our deepest desires, aspirations, and values, guiding us towards a life filled with purpose and meaning.

Setting an intention is a profoundly personal and meaningful practice that involves clarifying your purpose and guiding your actions towards a specific outcome. When setting an intention, it's important to express it in a way that resonates with you and reflects your deepest desires and values.

Setting intentions with children involves using language that is simple, positive, and age-appropriate.

1. "Let's listen to our feelings and talk."
2. "we are going to have fun and learn something new today."
3. "May we use our words to build each other up and spread kindness."
4. " May I embrace creativity and imagination, finding joy in artistic expression and playful exploration."
5. "May we create a safe and welcoming environment where everyone feels included and valued."

Here are some examples of phrases you can use as an adult to set intentions:

1. "I set the intention to practice self-compassion and kindness towards myself and others."
2. "I set the intention to listen to my body and honour its needs with love and care."
3. "I intend to let go of what no longer serves me and embrace positive change."
4. "Today, I set the intention to practice forgiveness and release any resentment or anger weighing me down."
5. "May my heart be open, and may I approach each interaction with love, compassion, and empathy."

Create your own intentions and tailor them to your unique journey and aspirations. The key is to express your intentions authentically and from the heart, setting the stage for a meaningful and transformative grounding practice.

Incorporating Intentions into Grounding Practices:

Incorporating intentions into grounding practices involves infusing each moment with purpose and mindfulness. Whether engaging in mindful breathing, visualisation, or sensory awareness exercises, setting intentions permeate each action with a sense of significance and meaning. By consciously directing our attention and energy towards our intentions, we cultivate a more profound understanding of presence and connection with ourselves and the world around us.

Reflection and Adaptation:

As we embark on our grounding journey, it's essential to periodically reflect on our intentions and adapt them to align with our evolving needs and circumstances. Life is fluid and ever-changing, and our intentions must grow in tandem with our growth and experiences. By remaining open to new insights and perspectives, we ensure that our grounding practices remain relevant and effective in supporting our overall well-being.

In conclusion, the chapter on "Setting Intentions: The Foundation of Grounding" illuminates the pivotal role intentions play in anchoring us to the present moment and guiding our journey towards inner peace and stability. Through the lens of intention-setting, we gain clarity, purpose, and direction, transforming our grounding practices into profound opportunities for growth and healing.

By cultivating clarity of intention, we align our thoughts, emotions, and actions with our deepest desires and values, fostering a sense of purpose and meaning in our lives. Crafting meaningful intentions empowers us to confront our fears, embrace our vulnerabilities, and aspire towards the highest expression of ourselves.

Incorporating intentions into our grounding practices infuses each moment with mindfulness and significance, enabling us to cultivate a deeper connection with ourselves and the world around us. Through reflection and adaptation, we ensure that our intentions remain relevant and responsive to our evolving needs and circumstances, guiding us towards greater resilience and well-being.

As we continue to harness the transformative power of intention-setting in our grounding journey, we unlock the potential to navigate life's challenges with grace, authenticity, and unwavering presence. With each intention we set, we affirm our commitment to living a life filled with purpose, passion, and profound inner peace.

Conclusion: Grounded: A Comprehensive Guide to Grounding Techniques for Children and Adults

As we reach the conclusion of this journey through grounding techniques for children and adults, it's essential to reflect on the profound impact that these practices can have on our well-being. Grounding is not just a collection of exercises but a transformative approach to living a more balanced and centred life.

In the hustle and bustle of our modern world, filled with constant stimuli and demands, the simple yet powerful act of grounding provides a refuge—an anchor that helps us navigate the storms of stress, anxiety, and uncertainty. We've explored a variety of techniques, from the fundamental breathwork and mindfulness exercises to the playful activities that reconnect us with the beauty of our senses and the natural world.

For children, grounding becomes a magical journey of self-discovery and resilience-building. Through creative and age-appropriate activities, they learn not only to manage their emotions but also to embrace the wonders of imagination and play. These foundational skills become the stepping stones for a future where they can face life's challenges with courage and adaptability.

For adults, grounding is a lifeline—an invaluable tool in the pursuit of mental clarity, emotional stability, and physical well-being. Whether finding solace in a quiet moment of meditation, stretching our bodies through yoga, or immersing ourselves in the healing embrace of nature, these practices empower us to face our daily lives with greater mindfulness and purpose.

As you close the pages of this book, remember that grounding is not a one-size-fits-all solution. It is a personal and evolving journey. Embrace the techniques that resonate most with you, integrate them into your daily routine, and celebrate the small victories along the way. Consistency is the key to reaping the full benefits of grounding in your life.

In a world that often pulls us in different directions, grounding becomes a gift we give to ourselves, a deliberate act of self-care and self-love. It is a testament to our commitment to living authentically, present in each moment, and resilient in the face of life's challenges. May this book serve as a guide, a companion, and a source of inspiration on your ongoing journey towards a more grounded, balanced, and fulfilling life.

Appendix:

100 grounding experiences linked to Body, Breathing, self-soothing, distraction, observing, 80 affirmations, and 20 intentions

20 grounding exercises for the body

1. Yoga Poses for Grounding:

    Practice grounding yoga poses, such as Mountain Pose, Child's Pose or Warrior Pose.

    Child's Pose:

    1. Begin by kneeling on the floor with your knees hip-width apart and your big toes touching behind you.

    2. Lower your torso forward, bringing your forehead to rest on the floor in front of you while extending your arms forward or resting them alongside your body with palms facing up.

    3. Relaxation:

    - Hold the pose for several breaths, allowing your body to relax and sink deeper into the stretch with each exhale. Focus on breathing deeply into your back, feeling the expansion with each inhale, and the release with each exhale.

    - To release the pose, gently walk your hands back towards your body, lifting your torso upright and returning to the starting position on your hands and knees.

    Remember to listen to your body and modify the pose as needed to ensure comfort and safety. Child's Pose can be a soothing posture when you need a moment of rest and relaxation.

2. Neck Rolls:

    Neck rolls can help alleviate tension in the neck and shoulders:

    1. Start with a Neutral Position: Begin in a comfortable seated or standing position with your spine tall and your shoulders relaxed.

2. Roll Your Neck:
- Slowly tilt your head to the right, bringing your right ear towards your right shoulder, feeling a stretch along the left side of your neck.
- Then, gently roll your head forward, bringing your chin towards your chest, and continue rolling to the left so your left ear moves towards your left shoulder, stretching the right side of your neck.
- Complete the circle by rolling your head back, bringing your chin towards the ceiling, and returning to the starting position.

3. Jaw Relaxation:

To relax the jaw, you can perform a simple exercise to release tension.:

1. Open Your Mouth: Begin by sitting or standing comfortably with your spine tall and shoulders relaxed. Take a deep breath in through your nose.
2. Relax the Jaw: As you exhale, gently open your mouth wide while simultaneously relaxing your jaw muscles. Allow your lower jaw to hang loosely and naturally without clenching or tensing. You can gently wiggle your jaw from side to side or make small circles with your jaw to further release tension.

4. Body Tapping:

Body tapping, also known as "tapping therapy" or "tapping meditation," is a self-help technique that involves using your fingertips to gently tap on specific points of the body. It's often used to relieve stress and anxiety and promote relaxation:

1. Find a Quiet Space: Choose a quiet and comfortable space where you can relax without distractions.

2. Assume a Comfortable Position: Sit or stand comfortably with your feet shoulder-width apart and your arms relaxed at your sides.

3. Begin Tapping:
- Start by using your fingertips to gently tap on the following areas of your body, using a light to moderate pressure
- Top of the head: Use your fingertips to tap gently on the crown of your head.
- Eyebrows: Tap gently on the inner edges of your eyebrows near the bridge of your nose.
- Sides of the eyes: Tap gently on the bony ridge alongside your eyes.

- Under the eyes: Tap gently on the area beneath your eyes, just above your cheekbones.
- Under the nose: Tap gently on the area between your nose and upper lip.
- Chin: Tap gently on the area between your lower lip and chin.
- Collarbone: Tap gently on the area where your collarbones meet your chest.
- Under the arms: Tap gently on the sides of your body, just beneath your armpits.
- Top of the hands: Tap gently on the tops of your hands near your fingers.

4. Repeat: Continue tapping on each point for 5-10 taps or as long as it feels comfortable. You can repeat the sequence several times if desired.

5. Focus on Breathing: As you tap, focus on taking slow, deep breaths in through your nose and out through your mouth. Allow yourself to relax and release any tension with each exhale.

6. Check-In: After completing the tapping sequence, take a moment to check in with yourself and notice how you feel. Pay attention to any changes in your body or mood.

Body tapping can be done anytime, anywhere, and can be a helpful tool for managing stress and promoting relaxation. Experiment with different tapping sequences and adjust the pressure to find what works best for you.

5. Body Scan:

Sit or lie down comfortably.

Pay attention to each body part, starting from your toes and moving up to your head. Release tension as you go.

6. Tension Release:

Tense and then release different muscle groups. Start with your toes and work your way up to your head.

7. Hug Yourself:

Cross your arms and hug yourself, focusing on the sensation of touch and comfort.

8. Balancing Exercises:

   Stand on one leg for 30 seconds, then switch to the other. Focus on maintaining balance.

9. Progressive Muscle Relaxation (PMR):

   Tense and then relax specific muscle groups, one at a time. Notice the difference between tension and relaxation.

10. Shoulder Shrug and Release:

    Lift your shoulders toward your ears, hold briefly, and then release.

11. Balancing on One Leg:

    Stand on one leg for balance. Switch to the other after 30 seconds.

12. Rooting Exercise: Imagine roots growing from the soles of your feet into the earth, grounding you and providing stability

13. Mindful Walking:

    Take a slow, deliberate walk, paying attention to each step.

14. Grounding Stretches:

    Stretch your arms overhead, reach for your toes, or do simple neck and shoulder stretches.

15. Tactile Grounding

    Sensory Bin Fun: Explore a sensory bin with different materials.

    - Choose Your Base Material: Fill the plastic bin or container with your chosen sensory material. You can use one type of material or mix different ones for variety.
    - Add Objects: Place various objects and toys into the sensory bin. These items can vary in texture, size, and shape to provide a diverse sensory experience.
    - Explore: Encourage the child to explore the sensory bin with their hands. They can scoop, pour, sift, and bury objects in the material, engaging their sense of touch and proprioception.
    - Describe Sensations: Prompt the child to describe how the materials feel using descriptive words such as "soft," "gritty," "smooth," or "rough." Encourage them to notice the temperature, weight, and texture of the items.

- Encourage Play: Allow the child to engage in open-ended play with the sensory bin. They can use their imagination to create stories, build structures, or simply enjoy the tactile sensations.
- Mindful Observation: Encourage the child to practice mindfulness by focusing on the sensations they experience while interacting with the sensory bin. They can pay attention to the sound of materials shifting, the feeling of objects in their hands, and the visual patterns created as they play.
- Clean-Up: After playtime, help the child tidy up by returning objects to the sensory bin and storing them in a safe place for future use.

16. Sensory Awareness Techniques

    Nature Connection: Spend time outdoors, paying attention to nature sights, sounds and sensations.

17. Mindfulness and Meditation

    Guided Visualization: Imagine inhaling positive energy and exhaling stress.

18. Additional Techniques

    Imaginary Beach: Imagine being on a beach, feeling the sand, and hearing the waves.

19. Balance and Stability:

    Heel-to-Toe Walk: Take slow steps, placing the heel of one foot against the toe of the other.

20. Mindful Eating:

    Savouring Bite: Eat a small piece of food slowly, paying attention to taste, texture, smell and what it looks like.

20 grounding exercises for Breathing

1. Diaphragmatic Breathing:

   Inhale deeply through your nose, expanding your diaphragm.

   Exhale slowly through your mouth. Repeat several times

2. Box Breathing:

   Inhale for a count of 4, hold for 4, exhale for 4, and pause for 4. Repeat.

   Children may not be able to hold their breath for the count of 4 so you may need to alter this number.

   As you count, you may want to use an intention, so you might want to say one, let me be happy, 2, let me be calm and so on.

3. Alternate Nostril Breathing:

   Close one nostril with your thumb and inhale through the other.

   Close the other nostril and exhale through the open one. Repeat.

4. Breath Awareness:

   Focus on your breath. Notice the sensation of each inhale and exhale.

5. Breath and Movement Coordination:

   Coordinate breath with simple movements, like raising your arms on inhale and lowering on exhale.

6. Body Awareness Meditation:

   Sit comfortably and bring your attention to your breath.

   Gradually expand your awareness to the sensations in different parts of your body.

7. Balloon Breathing:

   Inhale slowly and deeply, imagining your lungs as a balloon expanding.

   Exhale slowly, visualising the balloon deflating. Repeat.

8. Sighing Breath:

   Inhale deeply through your nose.

   Exhale audibly with a sighing sound, releasing tension.

9. Deep Belly Breathing:

    Inhale slowly through your nose, allowing your diaphragm to expand.

    Exhale slowly through your mouth, feeling your belly contract. Focus on the breath and repeat.

10. Breath Focus Meditation:

    Sit comfortably and focus on your breath.

    Notice the sensation of each inhale and exhale, gently bringing your attention back if it wanders.

11. Humming Breath:

    Inhale deeply and exhale with a humming sound. Feel the vibration in your chest.

12. Counting Breaths:

    Count each breath, starting over if your mind wanders. Aim for a specific count, like 10 breaths.

13. Star Breathing:

    Inhale along one arm, hold at the top, exhale down the other arm, and pause at the bottom.

14. Pursed Lip Breathing:

    Inhale through your nose, exhale through pursed lips. This can help with anxiety.

15. Feather Breaths:

    Inhale gently as if you're lifting a feather, and exhale slowly, keeping the imaginary feather afloat.

16. Lotus Breath:

    Inhale as you imagine a lotus flower opening. Exhale as it closes.

17. Bhramari (Bee Breath):

    Inhale deeply and exhale while making a humming sound like a bee.

18. Bamboo Breathing:

    Inhale slowly, imagining your spine as flexible as bamboo. Exhale, releasing tension.

19. Colour Visualization:

    Inhale a calming colour, exhale any stress or tension as a different colour.

20. Ocean Breath:

    Inhale deeply, then exhale with a soft "haaa" sound, mimicking ocean waves.

20 Grounding Exercises for self-soothing:

1. Gentle Self-Touch:

    Place your hand over your heart or on your belly.

    Feel the warmth and comfort of your touch.

2. Positive Affirmations:

    Repeat positive affirmations to yourself, such as "I am safe" or "I can handle this."

3. Imaginary Safe Place:

    Close your eyes and imagine a peaceful and safe place.

    Visualize the details and immerse yourself in the calming environment.

4. Soft Music or Sounds:

    Listen to soothing music or nature sounds.

    Allow the sounds to create a calming atmosphere.

5. Cuddling with a Soft Object:

    Hold onto a soft, comforting object like a plush toy or a blanket.

    Feel the texture and let it bring a sense of security.

6. Warm Bath or Shower:

    Take a warm bath or shower, focusing on the sensation of water.

    Imagine stress washing away with each drop.

7. Aromatherapy:

    Use calming scents like lavender or chamomile.

    Inhale deeply and let the aroma soothe your senses.

8. Mindful Tea Drinking:

    Prepare a cup of herbal tea.

    Sip slowly, paying attention to the warmth and flavour.

9. Soothing Visualization:

   Close your eyes and visualise a gentle, calming light surrounding you.

   Imagine it gradually spreading peace throughout your body.

10. Comfortable Clothing:

    Put on soft, comfortable clothing that makes you feel at ease.

11. Connection:

    Spend time in nature, whether it's a walk in the park or sitting under a tree.

    Focus on the sights, sounds, and sensations around you.

12. Mindful Journaling:

    Write down your thoughts and feelings.

    Express yourself without judgment.

13. Calming colours:

    Surround yourself with calming colours like blues and greens.

    Allow the colours to evoke a sense of tranquillity.

14. Loving-Kindness Meditation:

    Send thoughts of love and kindness to yourself.

    Repeat phrases like "May I be happy, may I be at peace."

15. Positive Affirmations:

    Repeat positive affirmations to yourself. For example, "I am calm and in control" or "I can handle this."

16. Comforting Touch:

    Place your hand over your heart or give yourself a gentle hug.

    Feel the warmth and comfort of your own touch.

17. Sensory Grounding: Engage your senses by focusing on specific sensory experiences, such as the feeling of textures, the taste of a soothing drink, or the scent of calming essential oils.

18. Soothing Sounds:

    Listen to calming music, nature sounds, or white noise.

    Pay attention to the soothing qualities of the sounds.

19. Gentle Movement:

    Engage in slow, gentle movements, such as rocking back and forth or swaying side to side.

    Focus on the rhythmic and calming nature of the movement.

20. Self-Compassion Practice:

    Speak to yourself with kindness and understanding.

    Acknowledge your feelings without judgment.

20 grounding exercises for distraction

1. Colouring Book:

   Engage in colouring to shift your focus.

2. Cloud Watching:

   Find a comfortable spot and observe the shapes of clouds.

3. Nature Sounds:

   Go outside or listen to recordings of nature sounds to create a calming atmosphere.

4. White Noise:

   Use white noise to create a neutral background sound.

5. Fidget Toys:

   Use fidget spinners, cubes, or other tactile toys.

6. Play-Doh:

   Engage in sculpting or modelling with Play-Doh.

7. Memory Game:

   Challenge yourself with a memory game.

8. Counting Backwards:

   Count backwards from 100 by increments of 3 or any other chosen number.

9. Name Game:

   Pick a category (e.g., fruits, movies) and list items alphabetically. Alternatively, pick a number that corresponds with the alphabet, so the number five would be the letter E, and then pick five things that begin with the letter E.

10. 5-4-3-2-1 Technique:

    Name 5 things you can see, 4 things you can touch, 3 things you can hear, 2 things you can smell, and 1 thing you can taste.

11. Colour Scanning:

    Look around and name all the items you see of a specific colour.

12. Describe Your Surroundings:

   Use detailed language to describe the environment around you, including colours, shapes, and textures.

13. Engage in a Puzzle:

   Work on a crossword puzzle, Sudoku, or any other type of puzzle.

14. Name Your Emotions:

   Identify and name the emotions you're currently feeling.

15. Mindful Observation:

   Choose an object and observe it in detail, noticing colours, shapes, and patterns.

16. Hum a Tune:

   Hum or sing a familiar tune, focusing on the rhythm and melody.

17. Doodle or Draw:

   Create simple doodles or drawings on a piece of paper.

18. Grounding Objects:

   Carry a small grounding object in your pocket and focus on its texture when needed.

19. Affirmations:

   Repeat positive affirmations to shift your mindset.

20. Word Association:

   Start with a word and associate it with the first word that comes to mind. Continue the chain.

20 grounding exercises for observing

1. Pattern Recognition:

   Identify patterns in your environment, whether in nature, on a wall, or in your clothing.

2. Pebble Meditation:

   Hold a pebble and observe its texture, weight, and temperature.

3. Soundscapes:

   Close your eyes and focus on the sounds around you, distinguishing between different noises.

4. Leaf or Flower Observation:

   Study the details of a leaf or flower, noticing its colour, texture, and structure.

5. Observing Emotions:

   Notice and name your emotions as they arise, observing them without getting caught up in the story.

6. Wind Watching:

   Feel the wind on your skin and observe how it affects the movement of leaves and branches.

7. Observing Silence:

   Spend time in complete silence, observing the absence of noise.

8. Mirror Gazing:

   Look into a mirror and observe your reflection, paying attention to your expressions.

9. Lying on the Grass:

   Lie down on the grass and observe the shapes and patterns in the clouds or the movement of leaves.

10. Silent Observation:

    Spend a few minutes in silence, observing your surroundings without speaking.

11. Observing Your Thoughts:

   Sit quietly and observe your thoughts without getting attached to them. Let them come and go.

12. Technology Detox:

   Take a break from screens and observe the world around you without digital distractions.

13. Foggy Window Art:

   Huff on a window, then draw or write on the foggy window and observe the changes as it clears.

14. Stone Stacking:

   Stack stones or pebbles, observing the balance and stability of each layer.

15. Bubble Observation:

   Blow bubbles and observe their shapes, movements, and reflections.

16. Nature Observation:

   Spend time observing the details of plants, trees, or insects in a natural setting.

17. Gazing Meditation:

   Choose a point to gaze at and let your focus rest there, allowing thoughts to come and go.

18. Sound Scavenger Hunt:

   List and observe as many different sounds as you can hear in your environment.

19. Body Posture Awareness:

   Observe your own body posture and make adjustments for comfort and relaxation.

20. Time Perception:

   Observe your perception of time and how it changes in different situations.

40 affirmations in grounding work for children

1. I am like a strong tree with roots deep in the ground.

2. My feet are planted firmly, like seeds growing into big trees.

3. I am safe and secure in this moment, like a cosy hug.

4. I breathe in calmness and breathe out any worries.

5. Like a superhero, I can handle anything that comes my way.

6. I am as steady as a rock, strong and unshakable.

7. The ground supports me, just like a superhero's cape.

8. I trust in myself and the journey I'm on, like an adventurous explorer.

9. I let go of things that bother me, like balloons floating away.

10. I am as brave as a lion, facing challenges with courage.

11. My imagination is like a magic carpet taking me to happy places.

12. I am a shining star connected to the universe's bright energy.

13. I am a good friend, spreading kindness like sunshine.

14. I am a rainbow of emotions, each colour expressing how I feel.

15. I listen to my heart like a wise owl guiding me.

16. I am a puzzle piece, unique and important in the big picture.

17. I am like a butterfly, growing and changing with each new day.

18. I am as smart as a wise owl, always learning and growing.

19. My dreams are like seeds, growing into wonderful adventures.

20. I am a special part of my family, like a cherished treasure.

21. I am a kind and caring person, like a gentle breeze.

22. I am as bright as the sun, spreading warmth and joy.

23. I can do hard things, just like a determined ant carrying a big load.

24. I am like a flower, blooming with positivity and beauty.

25. I am a good listener, like a rabbit with big, attentive ears.

26. I am grateful for my body, like a happy, healthy bear.

27. I am as curious as a cat, exploring the world around me.

28. I am as strong as a mountain, facing challenges with strength.

29. I am like a rainbow fish, sharing my unique colours with the world.

30. I am like a scientist, learning and discovering new things.

31. I am a helper, spreading kindness like a friendly firefly.

32. I am like a shooting star, full of energy and enthusiasm.

33. I am a positive thinker, turning clouds into sunny skies.

34. I am a good sleeper, resting peacefully like a cosy teddy bear.

35. I am a creative artist, painting my world with bright colours.

36. I am as important as the moon and stars in the night sky.

37. I am a good problem solver, figuring things out like a clever fox.

38. I am a friend to animals, just like a gentle lamb.

39. I am a good sharer, like a considerate squirrel with its nuts.

40. I am as gentle as a breeze, treating others with kindness.

40 affirmations in grounding work for adults

1. I am grounded, rooted, and connected to the earth.

2. My body is a vessel, anchored in the present moment.

3. I trust in the natural flow of life and release what I cannot control.

4. Each breath I take fills me with calm and stability.

5. I am resilient, like the sturdy trunk of a tree in the wind.

6. The earth supports me, and I trust in its nurturing energy.

7. I release tension and embrace relaxation in every muscle.

8. My feet are firmly planted, grounding me in the here and now.

9. I am safe and secure in the embrace of the present moment.

10. Like a mountain, I stand tall, unshaken by life's challenges.

11. I am open to the wisdom and guidance of the earth beneath me.

12. I let go of worries, allowing them to flow away like leaves on a stream.

13. I am in harmony with the rhythms of nature and the universe.

14. My energy is balanced, flowing smoothly through me.

15. I choose peace over stress and let serenity fill my being.

16. I am a part of the universe, connected to all living things.

17. With every step, I am mindful of the ground beneath me.

18. I release fear and embrace the grounding power of love.

19. I trust the journey of life and surrender to its unfolding.

20. The earth supports my journey, and I am grateful for its stability.

21. I am present in my body, fully experiencing each moment.

22. Like the roots of a tree, I draw strength from my experiences.

23. I release negativity and invite positivity into my life.

24. My mind is clear, and my thoughts are grounded in reality.

25. I am centred, finding balance in the midst of chaos.

26. The protective energy of the earth surrounds me.

27. I let go of what no longer serves me, creating space for growth.

28. My spirit is grounded and connected to my inner strength.

29. I trust the process of life and embrace its lessons with gratitude.

30. I am a beacon of calmness, radiating peace to those around me.

31. I am in tune with the natural rhythms of the universe.

32. I release stress and welcome the soothing energy of the present.

33. My thoughts are grounded, and I approach challenges with clarity.

34. I am at peace with the past, present, and future.

35. I am a channel for positive energy, allowing it to flow through me.

36. Each breath grounds me deeper into the essence of who I am.

37. I am connected to the earth and honour its gifts.

38. I release attachment to negative thoughts and trust the journey ahead.

39. I am a force of positivity, radiating good energy into the world.

40. I am grounded, anchored, and secure in the embrace of the present.

10 intentions tailored for children:

1. "Today, I intend to be curious and explore the world around me with wonder and excitement."

2. "My intention is to be kind to my friends and classmates, and to always lend a helping hand."

3. "I set the intention to be brave and try new things, even if they seem scary at first."

4. "May I use my words to express my feelings and thoughts in a respectful and honest way."

5. "Today, I intend to learn something new and grow a little bit smarter every day."

6. "My intention is to take care of myself by eating healthy foods, getting enough sleep, and playing outside."

7. "May I find joy in the little things and appreciate the beauty in the world around me."

8. "I set the intention to be a good listener and show empathy towards others."

9. "Today, I intend to be mindful and take deep breaths when I feel upset or overwhelmed."

10. "My intention is to be grateful for my family, friends, and all the good things in my life."

These intentions are designed to empower children to cultivate positive habits, develop emotional intelligence, and foster a sense of gratitude and wonder in their daily lives.

10 intentions tailored for adults:

1. "Today, I intend to approach challenges with resilience and an open mind, knowing that I have the strength to overcome them."

2. "My intention is to cultivate inner peace and calmness amidst life's uncertainties, finding moments of stillness and tranquillity."

3. "I set the intention to prioritise self-care and nourish my mind, body, and spirit with activities that bring me joy and rejuvenation."

4. "May I practice gratitude daily, acknowledging the blessings in my life and finding appreciation in both big and small moments."

5. "Today, I intend to cultivate compassion and empathy towards myself and others, recognising our shared humanity and interconnectedness."

6. "My intention is to live authentically, embracing my true self and honouring my values in all aspects of my life."

7. "I set the intention to let go of negative thoughts and self-limiting beliefs, replacing them with positive affirmations and self-love."

8. "May I create meaningful connections and nurture supportive relationships, fostering a sense of belonging and community."

9. "Today, I intend to embrace change as an opportunity for growth and transformation, trusting in the journey and embracing new possibilities."

10. "My intention is to live with intention and purpose, aligning my actions with my goals and aspirations to create a life of fulfilment and meaning."

These intentions serve as guiding principles for adults to cultivate mindfulness, resilience, self-compassion, and personal growth in their daily lives.

Printed in Great Britain
by Amazon